COACHED For Success!

❖❖❖❖❖❖❖❖❖❖❖❖❖❖❖

The College Years

Seven Success Strategies...

for Millenials to Start and Finish

College in Four Years

Valerie Griffin
and Rishal Stanciel

ISBN-13: 9781451542936
ISBN-10: 1451542933

For this new generation of students, now more than ever, higher education is the ticket to upward mobility.

*Yet, far too many students
who start college never finish*

CONTENTS

- *College graduation rates*
- *Core college classes and skills*
- *"College Educated"*

Seven Success Strategies for Millennials to Start and Finish College

- *Cost of college*
- *Budgeting*
- *Credit cards*
- *Loans*

Research Insights:

- *Impact of attending college*
- *What you wish you had known and advice to high school students*
- *Three Things you struggled with in your 1st two years of college*
- *Insight from 1st generation college students*
- *The value of budgeting*
- *Value of taking math classes*
- *Leadership impact on campus*
- *Integrity: What is it?*
- *The impact of your personal brand*
- *Choosing your major and selecting a career path*

FOREWORD

Dear Students and Parents,

In working with talented students at colleges and universities across the country, we have been given a unique opportunity through coaching and mentoring to impact and change the lives of young people. As coaches, we primarily focus on self assessment, academic excellence, core skills development, relationship building, career preparation and life skills training.

We continue to work tirelessly and joyfully with students as we guide them through the most critical stages of their growth and development.

We have found our passion working with "Millennials." Millennials were typically born between 1982 and 1996 and are also referred to as "Generation Y". We define them as a generational cohort of individuals born in the 1980's and 1990's. They can be characterized by their incredible ability to multi-task, concern for work/life balance, impatience, team orientation, community involvement, need for affirmation and being the most ethnically diverse generation in our history. Texting is the preferred form of communication; they are the technology-driven generation. They are what we refer to as the "Jetson Generation" (derived from a cartoon about a futuristic family called the "Jetsons").

Yet, despite all the access to resources and people that technology affords, we have been saddened by the void in college preparation that we have witnessed in students across the nation. This lack of preparation carries over into their search for jobs resulting in frustration and many lost opportunities. In working with recruiters, we commonly hear that students are not focused, have not conducted the appropriate level of research, or acquired sufficient knowledge about the industry or position they are pursuing.

We have had the pleasure of watching the hundreds of students we have coached and mentored blossom. We witnessed a transformation in their lives. But we have only touched the tip of the iceberg. When we talk about what we do as coaches, the response is always the same, no matter where we go: "I wish I had a Coach!", "Can you help me?", "Would you help my son/daughter in college?"

Regrettably, we can only reach a limited population of students through one-on-one coaching. We have written this book to help students who are not fortunate enough to have a College Career Coach. We are sharing the lessons, experiences, wisdom and success strategies that elude so many. To successfully navigate "The College Years" requires personal characteristics we identify as the

"4 Ps" (Preparation, Performance, Persistence and Perception) that are integrated throughout our Seven Success Strategies.

If you implement the "Seven Success Strategies" outlined in this book, you can have *the time of your life, as you change your life*. Coached For Success! The College Years: Seven Success Strategies…for Millennials to Start and Finish College in Four Years will enable you to say you are truly "College Educated," Coached For Success!, and ready to successfully transition into the workplace.

Coach Valerie Griffin and Coach Rishal Stanciel

PREFACE

Today's environment presents so many wonderful opportunities and options for students that desire a college education. There are many different paths that can be taken to achieve your goals.

This is an exciting time particularly for the student that has done well academically, is mature, and disciplined. Your college selection should be governed by the size, type, location, reputation and cost of the institution. Students know thy self and be conscientious of thy parents' wallet. You have many choices and your challenge will be to find the school that best fits your needs, addresses some of your wants and will provide an environment that promotes your continued growth and success.

There are also great options available to the student whose academic performance, maturity or discipline would prohibit them from immediately attending a competitive college. Know your strengths and weaknesses. College represents a wonderful opportunity to reinvent yourself. Select an environment that will allow you to develop the best you. Another option is a college campus that is designed to provide structure for students that would otherwise flounder and return home with few college credits and a significant amount of student loan debt to show for the experience.

If you are unable to immediately attend college full-time, productive time can be spent working, gaining discipline and maturity while taking one or two courses to improve your study skills and academic performance. Working also provides independence and the ability to contribute to the cost of your education. For some, this can be the first step toward self-determination and the preparation needed prior to being a successful full-time student.

Students know that your parents desire the best for you. Most parents would like to send their son or daughter to the college of their dreams. They envision their child in an idyllic campus setting, making new friends, learning about the world and themselves and returning home with a degree and a job. However, know that your college decision should not be a sole function of where you ideally want to go to school but should ultimately be a decision made with your parents' involvement and agreement. Their financial circumstances should weigh heavily on your choice if they will be responsible for paying the tuition. Many parents are often crippled with guilt when they are not in a position to give their child what they want. This paralysis can often lead to making unwise choices. There has been a significant restructuring in the economy. Proceed with caution in deciding where and how much your parents can really afford to pay for your college tuition.

There are many circumstances where parents may not be equipped to decide where you should go to college and as a high school student, you aren't typically financially savvy enough to handle the responsibility of making such a choice. Take emotion out of the equation, become aware of options and alternatives and the selection process becomes simpler. The key is being informed. Appreciate that your parents have made good decisions allowing you to reach this point and now is not the time to tune them out or ignore their input and advice. Their wisdom and counsel is still needed and continuing your education is the right choice.

Yes, the income gap is widening between those with college degrees and those with only a high school education. This is one of many reasons to continue your education. The numbers are compelling. But we also want to create an awareness of other tangible and intangible benefits a college education and graduation affords. To give you a clear sense of these benefits, we asked 3rd and 4th year college students around the country to tell us the impact attending college has had on their ability to be successful. Here are some of their responses:

College has equipped me with multiple toolsets, skills, and a broadened perspective that is absolutely invaluable. Specifically, my reading comprehension, analytical skills, and writing abilities have increased tremendously.

3rd year Amherst student

College has changed me in too many ways to recount here. Some of the main changes have to do with my level of competence and confidence. The motto of my school is "work hard, play hard." You learn early on that success often means working hard and competing with others. My level of competence has risen exponentially because of the quality of my peers and the expectations of my professors, faculty, friends and mentors. Because of this, my confidence has also risen. I am more able to handle whatever comes my way. I feel like I can go up against the best of the best and still come out on top. I've come into contact with enough failures to be able to handle them, too.

4th year Duke Univ. student

College has taught me to evaluate what it means to be successful, through asking myself what I want out of life and how I am going to achieve it. I've also learned more about my personal skills and attributes, strengths and weaknesses. This has helped in understanding what I'm capable of doing as an individual.

4th year Harvard student

College has trained me to think deeper, ask the right questions, and be far more robust and still to the point while developing answers. The conversations that I have had with my peers pushed my intellectual capacity to new limits. All of this has contributed to my ability to handle any situation that might come and thus, my capacity for success is far greater than if I [had] not attended college, and more specifically the University of Chicago.

3rd year Univ. of Chicago student

I have been able to build great connections with people in my desired industry, to learn more about what I am capable of achieving, to understand the importance of giving back to the community, especially to members of my race, and also gain the intellect and analytical skills needed to be successful in society today.

3rd year Univ. of Southern CA student

I think college has made all the difference in that it has opened up many doors for me. Everyone today has a bachelor's degree, so it was kind of expected that I would go to college. However, college alone was not enough. I think being involved in other activities and being part of leadership/mentorship programs was also crucial.

4th year Stanford student

College has helped me become more independent and self sufficient and not so reliant on my parents. I chose to go to school across the country where I would be forced to handle problems (social, academic, financial, etc.) on my own. It has toughened me and better prepared me for the real world. I would say Morehouse has played a large role in this process as well.

3rd year Morehouse College student

Attending college has made all the difference in my journey to becoming a successful and independent member of society. I am the first person in my family to attend (and that will graduate from) a University. If I had not left my hometown, I would never have been exposed to all the opportunities that one can strive for beyond high school.

4th year Univ. of Texas, McComb student

College has helped me learn how to think about a question or problem, analyze data, and formulate an opinion about the situation. I also feel more confident about my ability to answer critical questions, or just converse with a professional, professor, or co-worker. I also feel as though I can pick up a book on any subject and learn the material. I think you can only do that well after college.

4th year NYU student

It helped me mature and get more focused on what I will do. It opened me up to the world that I didn't know existed in college. I understand that my reach can go further than I can even imagine. It's a stepping stone to law school.

3rd year Cornell Univ. student

INTRODUCTION

"Less than 55 percent of first-time students at the average four-year college graduate within six years, and at many institutions, students have less than a one in three chance of earning a degree—even as they spend thousands of dollars on tuition and accumulate thousands of dollars of debt."[1] While the overall graduation rates are low for all students, they are particularly low for minority and low-income students: only 46% of African American, 47% of Latino, and 54% of low-income new full-time freshmen graduate within six years. [2] "Our higher education system is a world class system and is a great asset to the general welfare and quality of our society," said Kevin Carey, Senior Policy Analyst. "But, it is failing to graduate the numbers of students needed if we are to continue to compete in a global economy."[3]

---

1   Carey, Kevin, Hess, Frederick M., Kelly, Andrew P., and Schneider, Mark, American Enterprise Institute Study: "*Diplomas and Dropouts: Which Colleges Actually Graduate Their Students (and Which Don't)*." (80 pages); Internet; accessed Jan. 2009.
2   Kevin Carey, The Education Trust Report: "*A Matter of Degrees: Improving Graduation Rates in Four-Year Colleges and Universities*." Internet accessed Dec. 2009
3   Ibid.

According to a *New York Times* article[4], only half of the students in the United States who enroll in college end up with a bachelor's degree. According to the U.S. Census Bureau,[5] workers with a bachelor's degree earned an average of $56,788 in 2006; those with a high school diploma earned $31,071. The impact can be more clearly seen when viewed in this table:

Education	Avg. Income	Increase
Drop-out	$20,873	—
High school	$31,071	48.9%
College	$56,788	82.8%
Advanced	$82,320	45.0%

You CAN achieve and enjoy the lifestyle that a college degree affords! Completing college is huge. Over a lifetime, a college degree is generally worth almost a million dollars. That's money that can be used for investing, traveling or whatever is important to you. The financial rewards of a college education are significant, and they're very real.

---

4   David Leon Hardt, *"Colleges are failing in graduation rates."* New York Times, Sept. 2009.
5   US Census Press Release, January 10, 2008.

Your goal is to graduate and proudly wear the label "College Educated." College educated can be defined as having:

- solid written and verbal communication skills

- aptitude to think critically, creatively and independently

- capability to analyze data and ask questions

- capacity to apply knowledge across multiple disciplines

- skills to function as a team member

- ability to cultivate and maintain relationships

- ability to act and think as a leader in group discussions

Why is this important? It is what employers demand of new hires. These are the skills you will need to be successful in life. This demands that you take some basic and fundamental classes, regardless of your major or school requirements:

- Overcome your fear of math. If your college does not require that you take any additional math courses, we advise you to take two or more math or other quantitative-based classes at the university level. This will allow you to obtain the following important skills:

  a) ability to identify and analyze patterns and see relationships
  b) logical, critical thinking and problem solving

- Develop quantitative proficiency and exposure through micro- and macro- economics, statistics or decision analysis.

- Take Business Writing classes. Employers demand that you possess excellent communication skills, both written and verbal. Punctuation, grammar and spelling may be a lost art, but employers still expect you to start your career armed with these skills. Writing skills are essential and will contribute to your success in any career field. Those who have these skills will realize the greatest success. Even in this electronic age, you will be called upon to write business letters, proposals, strategies, and business plans. Verbal communication skills will enable you to make persuasive arguments in the classroom and deliver your ideas effectively in campus organizations and ultimately in the workplace.

- Take accounting and/or finance classes. Accounting is the most basic framework of business, and finance is the backbone of business. It teaches you how to understand the financial position of a company and provides an understanding of budgeting from a corporate and personal perspective.

- Take courses that require formal individual and group presentations. Overcome your fear of public speaking by joining your local Toastmasters or other public speaking organizations.

- Become proficient in Word, Excel and PowerPoint. If you haven't already done so, take a typing class to improve your efficiency.

To round out your college experience:

- Acquire proficiency in a foreign language. This is a great way for you to further differentiate yourself in a competitive market. Language proficiency means that you can unexpectedly be interviewed in the language you profess to speak.

- Study abroad. It's hard to believe that only 1% of students from the US study abroad each year. Studying abroad provides a unique perspective when you are able to immerse yourself in another culture, its language and traditions. Become a part of this elite group to increase your competitiveness in the global marketplace.

- Make a decision to become a lifelong learner. No matter how smart you are, you will never know it all. This is an undisputable fact. Embrace change and grow.

CHAPTER 1

Take Control of Your Finances...debt today will affect lifestyle tomorrow and for years to come

Budgeting is important and necessary. It enables you to finish college on time and save money. Given 6 out of 10 students will take six years to graduate from college, the cost of two additional years can be staggering.

Total cost of attending college includes tuition, fees, room and board:
- In-state student at state college -- approx. $18K annually
- Out of state student at state college -- approx. $34K annually
- Private college -- approx. $48K annually

The significant cost of two additional years of school is huge. In the in-state example, it represents $36K of incremental costs and two years of lost wages. In the out-of state example, the number skyrockets to a whopping $68K and finally, staying an additional two years at a private college is a staggering $96K.

College	4 year Total Cost	6 year Total Cost	Increase in Cost 2 more years
In-State (state univ.) [6]	$72,000	$108,000	$36,000
Out of state (state univ.) [7]	$136,000	$204,000	$68,000
Private university [8] (regardless of residency)	$193,000	$289,000	$96,000

If you are fortunate to reside in a state that offers lottery funded or merit based scholarships, this can significantly impact your cost of attending college. These programs are designed to provide resources for talented students to attend public and private colleges or universities in their home state. A few of the states that offer these programs are: Georgia, Texas, Florida, Tennessee, Michigan, Nevada and South Carolina. This is an amazing resource and enables many students to graduate from great schools with little to no debt.

We are perplexed when we see students from financially challenged homes with parents that have very little retirement savings or investable assets make the decision to attend out of state schools. This is even more disconcerting when the out of state school isn't as competitive as their local universities and they reside in a state where merit based scholarships are available.

---

6   University of Georgia," Available from http://www.uga.edu. Internet: accessed Jan 2010.
7   Florida State University," Available from http://www.fsu.edu. Internet: accessed Jan 2010.
8   Cornell University," Available from http://www.cornell.edu .Internet: accessed Jan 2010.

It can become very difficult and impose a significant amount of stress on you and your parents when you attend a college your parents really can't afford. In some cases, the stress can result in health issues and estrangement from the family. This tends to increase your odds of not graduating and certainly may impact your ability to finish within the four prescribed years. There are many bright and focused students that start out strong and get derailed for a host of reasons. Financial woes usually play a significant role in delayed graduation or the failure to graduate.

Our advice is to attend the best college for **you** that **you** can afford!

In choosing a college to attend, you must consider that there is a **major difference** between in-state and out-of-state tuition and the financial burden attached to each. Paying for college is a significant financial undertaking. When deciding on the school to attend, substantial consideration should be given to its cost and your ability or inability to absorb that cost.

If you find that your finances are challenged, you may want to consider attending a community college where tuition is affordable and then transferring to the college or university of your choice. It is not where you start; it is how you finish! Grades matter.

We have worked with many students that started out in local or community colleges, performed well academically and successfully transitioned into competitive public and well known private universities. A particular student that comes to mind is a young man who attended a community college in the Pacific Northwest.

He performed exceptionally well academically and was involved in leadership positions on his campus. His counselor at the community college was very impressed with his performance and recommended that he apply to one of the more elite private schools in the Northeast. He had never heard of this college but trusted his counselor's advice and researched the school. He was stunned at the reputation of the school and that his counselor thought so highly of him. He applied, was accepted, and is maintaining a high level of academic performance (3.6 GPA) at this very selective, Liberal Arts College. In addition to being smart, he has excellent communication skills and the self confidence needed to allow him to fit comfortably into his new environment.

Once you decide on the college to attend and are committed to graduating in four years, proper budgeting will:

- Help you steer clear of exorbitant loans

- Preserve your credit

- Enable you to exercise self-control (needs vs. wants)

- Develop a lifestyle habit of being disciplined

- Avoid the pitfalls of making desperate decisions

Before arriving on your college campus, you must prepare a budget. This will include identifying your source(s) of income:

Parental Support
College Trust Fund
Grants
Scholarships
Work Study
Student Loans
Other income

You will need to net your expenses against your sources of income to determine your financial picture. It is important to factor in when your money is scheduled to come in and projected to go out.

Tuition and Fees
Books and Supplies
Housing
Utilities
Phone
Meals
Clothes
Car (note, gas, maintenance)
Insurance (car, apartment)
Credit Card Payments
Entertainment
Travel
Other Expenses

If you have a shortfall, we suggest that you try to reduce expenses, increase income, and have honest discussions with parents/financial aid officers.

Right now, I am studying abroad and budgeting is playing a huge role in my experience. Budgeting allows you to make calculated decisions which require discipline and maturity. When you begin to budget you start to prioritize necessities versus luxuries. Budgeting places a lot of things into perspective.

3rd year Amherst College student

I make sure to keep an Excel spreadsheet to monitor the costs that I incurred so not to go over my allocated amount for the month.

3rd year Univ. of GA student

It was fine until I decided to move off campus and become more responsible for my finances. My last year in college, I decided to use a monthly budget and the outcome was that I did not spend on unnecessary items as much.

4th year Univ. of Buffalo student

A note about credit cards

They are enticing but they risk robbing you of future financial stability:

- Avoid the pitfalls of overspending that can result from the use of credit cards

- Identify needs (functional) vs. wants, e.g., Honda vs. BMW.

- Don't fall victim to the feelings of immediate gratification credit cards can provide…do not spend limited resources on technology gadgets or take spring break vacations you really can't afford; you don't have to be nor should you want to be the campus fashion icon…do you really need that many pairs of shoes? How will the numbers change your life? They won't.

- Do not finance your lifestyle with credit cards. When using credit cards, you are creating a credit history that generates a credit score. Your credit score is routinely evaluated as a condition for internship/full-time employment. Large sums of debt and late payments can signal irresponsibility and inability to manage money and poor decision-making.

- Watch out for ATM/debit cards…do not pay for pizza or any other conveniences with your debit card. Withdraw cash and spend the cash…then you will see how quickly it goes and it will force you to curtail your spending because when it's gone…it's gone.

"Too many students are at risk of overpaying for college by pulling out credit cards to pay for textbooks or even part of their tuition bill, instead of using less expensive financial aid to cover these items," said Marie O'Malley, director of consumer research for Sallie Mae and author of the study.[9] "Students and families need to build a comprehensive budget ahead of time to cover not only tuition, but also other necessities like supplies and travel costs that contribute to the overall cost of college."[10]

Many college students seem to use credit cards to live lifestyles they can't afford. A significant percent of students incur finance charges because they cannot pay off their monthly balance.

The study also found that two-thirds of survey respondents said they had frequently or sometimes discussed credit card use with their parents. The remaining one-third, who had never or only rarely discussed credit cards with parents, were more likely to pay for tuition with a credit card and were more likely to be surprised at their credit card balance when they received the invoice.[11]

In February 2010 new credit card legislation was passed, essentially stating that if you are under 21, you will need a co-signer to obtain a credit card.

9   Sallie Mae's National Study of Usage Rates and Trends, "How Undergraduate Students Use Credit Cards," 2009
10   Ibid.
11   Ibid.

When I graduate I will have some money saved and I will be debt free. I have a credit card but I monitor my spending and I pay off the majority of what I owe each month. My collegiate experience with managing my finances helped me understand the importance of a budget and that money goes just as fast as you get it. Spend wisely.

3rd year Florida State Univ. student

I didn't really start thinking about budgeting in college until the end of my sophomore year. I spent too much money my freshman year because 1) I bought too many clothes and 2) I spent way too much on non-dining hall food, even while on campus. Budgeting is so important because becoming wealthy requires having the discipline to save and not use money to satisfy hedonistic tendencies. I wish I had taken a course on budgeting early in college or had a set limit on how much I could spend a week. Avoid having a credit card in college and always use cash in transactions. It's easy to become desensitized to costs when you just swipe a card and sign your name.

3rd year Stanford student

Eighty-four percent of undergraduates indicated they needed more education on financial management topics. In fact, 64 percent would have liked to receive information in high school and 40 percent as college freshmen.[12]

---

12   Sallie Mae's National Study of Usage Rates and Trends, "How Undergraduate Students Use Credit Cards," 2009.

It was fairly easy because I was able to appeal for more aid in order to make my college experience a little more affordable. I spoke directly to my financial aid officer a number of times on the phone before I ever enrolled in my university in order to make sure I was able to afford school.

3rd year Boston University student

I will owe a lot of money to the government from all of my college loans when I graduate. I am an Accounting/Finance major and I am learning the true value of interest and loans. It's a scary thing thinking about how I will be able to pay it all back when I graduate but hopefully my career will pay enough to take care of all that and more. This essentially is my goal in life.

3rd year St John's Univ. student

You should visit your financial aid office and develop relationships with Financial Aid personnel. They are an incredible resource and may be able to provide valuable insight to students. They hold the key to sources of aid and grants, and the steps to take to qualify for funds.

Student loans

The scoop on school "student" loans...It is not free money and must be paid back!

Be smart about debt[13]

Borrow directly from the government

One of the early achievements of the Clinton administration was the Direct Loan Program, which cut out the middleman altogether in favor of one-to-one correspondence between student and lender. If you can't get a Pell grant or some other kind of funding that doesn't need to be paid back, try to secure federal student loans before signing up for private loans.

Federal student loans come with numerous consumer protections and flexible options for repayment, including graduated payments, income-sensitive plans and consolidation, which stretch out the repayment period to lower the payments.

Know the lender

Students often turn to private loans after exhausting their federal student loan options. This happens more often these days because the maximum undergraduates can borrow through federal loan programs hasn't changed since 1992 and students become desperate to secure funds to remain in school.

However, some students never apply for federal loans. Anyone who fills out a Free Application for Federal Student Aid can qualify for federal student loans, regardless of need.

---

13   Ibid.

Know the rate

The first factor is what you borrow (principal), and the rest will be interest, what your lender is charging you, often by the day, to borrow it. The rate by which interest accrues could result in you spending years paying off the interest before even beginning to touch the principal. Negotiate as hard as you can for the lowest rate possible, and pay the biggest amounts you possibly can right out of the gate. The smaller the principal, the lower your interest portion becomes, and the faster you can pay it off.

Interest rates for direct government loans are typically in the low single digits, while interest rates from private lenders can vary significantly and run into the high double digits.

> **Example**: If you borrow $30,000 in student loans to help finance your education and you have a loan re-payment period of 10 years, your payments will be a function of your interest rate. If you borrow at a rate of 4%, 9%, or 14%, you will have a monthly payment of $304, $380, or $466, respectively.

Only borrow what you need. Borrowing more in total for your education than you expect to make the first year out of school is dangerous to your long-term financial health, because you will likely have trouble affording the payments. Students should know this before they sign up for an education that's beyond their means.

The search for need-based or merit scholarship monies should begin months before you apply for financial aid. In fact, college scholarship monies can be obtained as early as your sophomore year in high school. This will require diligence and persistence on your part. You should factor into your senior year schedule dedicated time reserved for researching scholarship funds. Once you begin college, each year, you will need to dedicate time to renew scholarships or scout out new sources. Significant amounts of scholarship monies go unused every year because students simply fail to apply for them. Do not focus solely on large scholarships. If you are able to secure multiple $500, or $1,000 scholarships, this can have a significant impact in reducing your debt load. Take note of deadlines in writing essays, obtaining recommendations and providing transcripts that will be required in the application process.

> **Example:** A student attends a prestigious college in the northeast. By the time she graduates, she will have amassed more than $100,000 in student loan debt. This student has performed exceptionally well academically. Her 3.8 GPA certainly qualifies her for merit based scholarships. Unfortunately, when her financial aid office directed her to a huge resource book and internet sites that contained scholarship information and opportunities, she felt overwhelmed and found it easier to apply for student loans. If she secured her loans at a favorable rate, let's say 6%, and her total loan amount is $100,000 she can anticipate monthly student loan payments of $1,110 per month for the next 10 years upon graduation. A monthly expense of this magnitude will place a heavy toll on her budget and significantly impact her lifestyle and ability to be self sufficient after graduation.

Financially I prepared for college by telling myself that I would do anything in my power to keep from taking out any loans, ever. I did this by applying for over 20 scholarships during my senior year of high school and in turn I was awarded 11 of them. I also filled out my FAFSA on Jan. 1 of each year and I am thankful to have qualified for so many grants.

3rd year Florida State Univ. student

I made sure that I submitted all of my financial aid paperwork early so that I would get the maximum amount of money that was available. I also applied for outside scholarships.

3rd year Dartmouth student

If my scholarship (in both the financial and academic sense of the word) maintains, I'll be debt free, without having to have pay any significant amount of money out of my own pocket to attend four years of college. I've learned that if you look hard enough and WORK hard enough, there are plenty of opportunities out there for the person who has what it takes to find them, get them, and keep them.

3rd year Fisk Univ. student

I would tell them [high school students] to find out how to get the best for your money's worth. I wish I had all the pertinent information to make my college experience the best one, but one that did not place me in a huge debt position. I would suggest that high school students look carefully into the financial aspects of the college they choose.

3rd year Simmons College student

To ease the financial burden of attending college, secure funds from all available sources (college funds, scholarships, parents, etc); make affordable loan choices; avoid high cost options such as credit cards and high interest rate private loans; and create a budget. Remain disciplined and consistent in applying these principles.

CHAPTER 2

Academic excellence must be pursued...Grades matter[14]

To the outside world, grades define who you are and the value people may place on you. Grades control access to scholarships, organizations, fraternities, sororities, internships, graduate school, and full time jobs.

As long as I kept my grades above a certain standard, I was able to avoid all the hustle and bustle that students around me dreaded. I had to perform above and beyond everyone else all the time. I began to see that from a financial perspective, GRADES WERE EVERYTHING and understood that I was saving huge sums of money by working to maintain scholarship eligibility. No loans, no grants, no debt, no bills to pay, no working for minimum wage, no work study for scraps - just a serious investment [in] good grades, applying for internships, and community service.

3rd year Fisk University student

---

14   GPA references are based on 4.0 scale.

If I had known that all 4 years of my undergraduate academic career would matter and that I would later want to apply to graduate school, I would have been more diligent in seeking out resources.

4ᵗʰ year Yale Univ. student

I recommend that you hit the ground running. I took things very lightly and let a lot of easy classes go away when I should have [been] building my GPA. That is what really hurt me in the long run.

4ᵗʰ year Northwestern Univ. student

Myth: If you did well in high school, you'll do well in college.

Reality: Just because you (a) took massive numbers of AP courses, (b) were on the honor roll every semester in high school, (c) won almost every high school award, or (d) did all of the above, does not mean that you're going to find your route through college paved with gold. The amount of work required and the level of skills needed to do well increase significantly when you transition from high school to college—especially if you didn't go to a college preparatory high school (something you might not figure out until you actually get to college and observe classmates who are more academically prepared and disciplined). College grades involve more than studying. They require balance, prioritization, time management, relationships and stamina. Many students arrive on campus lacking (college level) study skills. We also see students who have the prerequisite study skills earn below average grades in college because they fail to incorporate the appropriate amount of time to actually study.

Upper level college students shared with us the frustration and anger they experienced, particularly in their first year, when they found it difficult to work at the pace of their classmates. They felt intimidated in the classroom as they listened to other students make sound and persuasive arguments. As a result, they were uncomfortable contributing to class discussions and shied away from study groups. This compounded their problem since class participation is a percentage of their overall grade. They were "A" students in high school yet, they had written few, if any, papers that required extensive research and in-depth analysis. When writing papers, they were further aggravated by the number of re-writes and amount of time they had to invest in completing those papers.

It's a whole new level. In high school I practically never studied and got straight A's...that isn't the case for college. Get into great study habits early.

4th year Hamilton College student

I had a great transition health- and sleep–wise, just not so great grade-wise, as I felt I could have done better. I wish I had known how much studying was really necessary.

3rd year Columbia Univ. student

19

I wish I had known how important it is to simply get a good GPA. I would tell students in high school to never take more than one hard class each quarter. While it is important to challenge yourself, I think you learn how to be a better student when you only have one challenging class to focus on at a time. I would also suggest all students consider doing a humanities major to improve writing skills and your ability to articulate ideas. Being more skills-focused in college will help you feel as though you are getting more out of the experience and will help in selling yourself in the future.

3rd year Stanford student

I sought a lot of tutoring because I was not academically prepared for college level work.

3rd year Dartmouth student

Example: A student was extremely successful at her local high school and was accepted into multiple colleges. During her first semester at a top 10 college, she realized that she wasn't equipped with the proper study skills or academic background to be successful. She really struggled and questioned whether she was college material.   She shared that she had to work twice as hard to compensate for her lack of preparation by putting in more hours than her peers just to earn "B's." She worked extremely hard to develop collegiate level study habits and discipline but was never able to move her GPA beyond a 3.0. However, her tenacity, industry knowledge and ability to network and maintain relationships enabled her to secure an opportunity within her chosen industry.

If, at the end of the first week of school--or at any point in your collegiate career--you feel any level of inadequacy relative to your classmates and the ability to master the material, you need to reassess your study habits and institute changes that will allow you to effectively compete for a winning grade. Many students fail to understand the value of time. As a college student, you have the freedom to choose how you spend your time. Students often mistakenly believe that they can use time outside of the classroom to sleep late, play video games, surf the net, socialize with friends, and party. Sadly, when the first set of grades arrives, their GPA reflects this misuse of time. Exercise discipline and restraint. Structure your day. You must allocate time to study EVERYDAY! If you start your college career with a disappointing GPA, it can take years for your GPA to recover and sometimes it's difficult to improve it to a level that allows you to be competitive in securing internships, full time employment and entry into advance degree programs.

Here are some suggestions to incorporate into your study plan:

- Know your most effective learning style. There are three general types: visual learners utilize pictures and taking detailed notes; auditory learners benefit from lectures, discussions, reading aloud and using recording devices; and tactile/kinesthetic learners use a hands-on approach and need activity and exploration.

- Taking class notes is a MUST.

- Read textbooks or assigned materials and prepare effective summaries.

- Review notes and materials prior to every class.

- You may want to utilize technology to record lectures or your own study notes.

- Make notes of materials you don't understand and consult with the professor, TA or classmates for clarity.

- Find conducive environments for studying (library, dorm room, etc.).

Myth: I'm not good at math and it isn't all that important. I'll never need to use it again.

Reality: The truth of the matter is that most individuals CAN do well in math. Attitude is everything. Maintaining a positive attitude is the first step to success. In today's information age, mathematics is needed more than ever. Problem solving skills are highly prized by employers today. Math requires knowing when and how to use the tools to assist in the problem solving process.

College level math coursework enables you to develop an understanding of and comfort in dealing with numbers and data, which provides a great foundation for analytical work. It requires consistent coursework in this area. Don't just take one math class! You can supplement your math coursework with courses that will enable you to apply your math skills.

Math is an essential foundation for any career path. More and more corporations are requiring logic and/or analytical based assessments as conditions of employment. Employers use these assessment tests as predictors of job performance.

If you think we are being redundant, **we are**! A firm understanding of basic math through College Algebra should equip you with the necessary analytical skills required to succeed in the workplace.

Math has been extremely helpful in my overall education. I would argue it has been the most important part of my education. Quantitative skills are also a prerequisite for just about any company that hires. I would recommend taking as many math courses freshman and sophomore year as possible so you build a good foundation for other subjects. Between freshman and sophomore year, I took 8 courses in math (about a full year): Calculus I, II, III, Linear Algebra, Multi-variable Calculus, Linear Optimization, Actuarial Modeling, Statistics I & II.

4th year NYU student

I've taken four math courses. They actually came in handy in other classes that have nothing to do with math, which is surprising because I figured I'd never revisit the material again.

4th year Univ. of GA student

I have taken 3 formal math courses, but all of my accounting and business classes have a math component to a certain extent. These classes have enhanced by analytical skills and helped me become a good problem solver.

3rd year Univ. of Southern CA student

I have taken 5 math courses. Math has developed my reasoning and problem solving skills in an almost subconscious way. Math allows your mind to always be ready to solve a problem methodically or at least to try to solve it methodically.

4th year Stanford student

Myth: If you work hard, you will do well in college.

Reality: Yes, you need to work hard to do well in college, but working hard is not enough in itself. You also have to produce good-quality work/papers and do well on the exams to get good grades in college. In college, it's the final product that counts.

Understand that you can invest a significant amount of time and energy studying and writing papers. However, effort does not equate to productivity and good grades. No matter how hard you may have worked on that paper, if it contains mistakes, doesn't have a clear point, or doesn't answer the question, it's not going to get a good grade. Be sure your definition of working hard measures up to the standards of your professors. To ensure success in your classes, there are study guides and resources materials you can purchase that will help you prepare and organize class notes; develop the organization skills needed to write papers; and study for tests.

> **Example:** A third year college student works very hard but hasn't realized his full potential. He neglects to utilize available campus resources such as: professor office hours, study groups, teaching assistants, tutors, or peer assistance. While he knows what he should do (because it has been clearly pointed out to him by mentors) he is unable to break the "Lone Ranger" syndrome. He realizes the need for a support system but has yet to create one. However, many students who work hard and avail themselves of peer and professor relationships typically experience improved academic performance. Even though he is from an Ivy League school known for its difficult coursework, having a 3.1 GPA renders him a weaker candidate in competing for internships.

The landscape has changed significantly. The stakes for obtaining superior grades are much higher. The minimum GPA for most industries is a 3.0. When trying to obtain opportunities with industry leaders (e.g. Coca Cola, Goldman Sachs, Google, Kraft, McKinsey, Microsoft, Pepsi), expectations are higher. Investment banking and consulting firms typically command minimum GPAs of 3.5 and higher.

Be aware that a strong (3.4) GPA can overcome the disadvantages that may be associated with a lesser-known university. A superior GPA (3.7) can be a point of distinction. A student with a 3.7 GPA at an average university can effectively compete for positions at top tier firms against a 3.0 student from a more prestigious college. Employers look for evidence of academic rigor and use the GPA to weed out underperformers and reduce the applicant pool. If you attend a top university, the inability to satisfy minimum GPA requirements will be a barrier to job opportunities with certain employers. Your GPA demonstrates to an employer that you have the ability to learn, manage time, possess technical skills, are motivated, and determined to succeed.

You cannot solely rely on the reputation of your university to compete in the job market. There will be many students from your school that will earn 3.5 GPAs and above. You must have superior academic performance, regardless of the reputation of your university. Grades matter!

Your competition is stiff, even on your own campus. There are more students earning GPAs of 3.5 and higher than there are employment opportunities. According to a survey from The National Association of Colleges and Employers, the groups' 2009 student survey found that just 19.7% of 2009 graduates who applied for a job actually have one.[15] In comparison 26% of those graduating in 2008 and 51% of those graduating in 2007 had a job in hand by the

---

15   Behman, John. "Got Work? College Graduates Face Toughest Market in Years." Available from http://www.abcnews.go.com/Business/story, Internet; accessed Jan. 2010.

time of graduation.[16] This represents a tremendous shift in available employment opportunities. As job prospects have dimmed, employers have become more selective in their choice of candidates. To ensure time is invested in qualified candidates, employers have implemented a number of screens to narrow the applicant pool. Cover letters, minimum GPA requirements, phone screens, writing samples, logic tests, and specific skills or course work are closely analyzed to identify candidates that fit their requirements. You must also add enthusiasm to these qualities. Hiring decisions are often based on both fit and enthusiasm.

Now that we have convinced you of the importance of grades, MAKE a decision to get the winning grades to open the door to career opportunities you desire.

Steps to Getting the winning grade (simple steps that many students fail to take):

1. Manage TIME! Time is the great equalizer. No one has any more hours in their day than you do. How you use your time determines your success or failure. Create a daily schedule that allocates time for your personal morning routine, classes, homework/studying, exercise, meals, social/organizational activities, laundry and sleep. Blocking out time for all of these activities will quickly alert you to how little time you actually have and when you have overcommitted.

---

16   Ibid.

2. Get a planner or Personal Digital Assistant (PDA) to keep track of classes, appointments, exams, projects... your life. Develop a plan and work the plan.

3. Buy your books immediately...professors assign homework the 1st week of class.

4. Scout out the location of each class before the 1st day. Many students arrive late and frustrated on the first day because they assumed they knew where the class was being held and invariably got lost.

5. Arrive for classes on time...throughout the entire course!

6. Always GO to classes—professors notice and it reinforces discipline!

7. Sit in the front of the class and be an active participant. This is a sure way to get the attention of the professor in a positive way. It gives the impression that you actually want to be there.

8. Take NOTES: Utilize your laptop or a spiral notebook, which can be invaluable...pages stay together and become your little bible for every class.

9. Join study groups immediately to maximize learning opportunities. Don't go it alone. Enlist the help of student groups, tutors, teaching assistants, professors and writing labs. This is not the place

where everyone on the team gets a trophy. You will receive the grade you earn.

10. Manage perceptions. Do not bring food to class, talk to your neighbor or text while in class. Let your behavior signal that you are in class to LEARN.

11. Get a tutor at the first sign of difficulty. It is important that you master the material. Your transcript only reveals your grade, not the steps you had to take to get the grade.

12. Utilize the professor's/teaching assistant's office hours...that's why they have them. They actually want you to come and get the help you need. If you are on the borderline between two grades, you can often receive the higher because of this effort. Arriving before class or staying after class to speak with your professor is another effective way to obtain the help you need.

13. Manage your course load. Create balance in your academic load...do not take all quantitative or qualitative classes in any given semester or quarter...Mix it up. An example of a balanced load might include math, history, sciences, and English. Managing this process well can impact your GPA. It is imperative that you seek advice from your academic advisors and upper classmen for help in selecting the right blend and sequencing of classes.

14. Know your school's add/drop policy and make changes in the first week of school to avoid falling behind.

15. Do not over-commit (classes, organizations, work, internships, family) — "NO" is an acceptable answer.

16. Manage pledging, partying, boyfriend/girlfriend relationships. There is nothing inherently wrong with any of these activities; however, timing and balance are key in avoiding the pitfalls.

17. Know and respect your body: Exercise, rest and eat well.

What if you are not an "A" student?

We cannot stress the importance of grades and encourage you to strive for the best grades possible but we also realize not everyone can or will earn GPA's of 3.5 and higher. Yet, you can effectively compete and distinguish yourself by completing the steps outlined above and focusing on what you can absolutely control. The 4P's: preparation, performance, persistence, and creating positive perceptions are the tools that will enable you to succeed in and outside of the classroom. When applying for internships, fellowships, scholarships or development programs, your transcript will be examined with an eye on identifying upward trends in grades. Courses you have taken will be reviewed and evaluated based on difficulty, type, and suitability of classes. Academic rigor will be assessed with a focus on quantitative and analytical skill development. If you want to take courses that will be beneficial to your development but concerned about the grades you will earn, you can take those courses at your community or local college. As transfer credits, they will not factor into your GPA.

Everyone has an area of strength and interest. Focus on the courses that you find intellectually stimulating and the ones you enjoy and give it your best. You will find it easier to earn the grades you desire in these courses. However, make sure these courses are useful in your quest for employment. After you identify your strengths, build on them. Take classes that enhance these skills and find organizations that will provide a platform to put them into action. Your genuine interest in a subject matter will enable you to develop more in-depth knowledge and stronger relationships with professors. Great relationships with professors will position you to take advantage of many leadership and internship opportunities.

Seek out leadership development programs. These programs will provide the one-on-one focus needed to further your development. You can find out about development programs through campus organizations, specific academic departments, fraternities/sororities or corporate websites. You can also use Google as a search engine to identify available programs. Participation will give you access to industry professionals who can help you hone the skills that will enable you to distinguish yourself and succeed.

Identify careers that will allow you to capitalize on your strengths. Realize that many successful people were not necessarily the highest academic achievers but they supplemented their academic performance with other strengths such as: great sales skills, excellent oral and written communication skills, expertise on specific subject matters, dependability, strong work ethic, or impressive analytical skills. Others found success being incredibly adept at working within teams.

You will need to operate at a heightened level of awareness and productivity to secure desired opportunities on and off campus. Determination, reliability, and relationship building are vital skills you must develop. Confidence will enable you to overcome many hurdles and help you win over skeptics. See yourself as a winner and surround yourself with others who have goals and are achieving them. Grades are not the sole predictor of success. Employers look for students that are well rounded, mature, disciplined, possess good communication and leadership skills. They want the complete package.

> **Example:** A student attends a top tier university and has a GPA below 3.0. He's a biomedical engineering major. He is interested in the financial services arena where there is a minimum 3.2 – 3.5 GPA requirement for top tier firms. Yet, this student was able to secure a great internship when others with significantly higher GPA's were not successful. Despite lower than average grades, this student was tenacious, well prepared and armed with industry knowledge, aggressive, outspoken, genuinely interested in financial services, funny, and likeable. He did not rely solely on campus recruiting but utilized his networking skills to make contact with industry

professionals. He was able to present and sell himself so effectively that his grades did not derail him. Yes, a biomedical engineering student is presumed to be smart, but he needed all the other attributes identified to overcome a low GPA.

Example: A student attended an Ivy League college had a 3.3 GPA and some leadership involvement on campus. By most accounts she would be considered a success story given the prestige of her college and a solid GPA. However, she couldn't effectively present herself and communicate the strengths of her candidacy. She secured a job with a second tier firm in a less than impressive position. She failed to showcase how her experiences in and out of the classroom positioned her as an effective leader. Weaknesses in her interviewing skills, industry knowledge and self confidence rendered her ineffective in competing with students on her campus and at lesser known colleges.

In a difficult job market students will need to investigate both traditional and nontraditional opportunities where their GPA is only one of the many selection factors used by employers. A career in sales is a great path to consider. Sales positions in pharmaceuticals, business services, communications, and retail financial services (insurance, banks, mortgage companies) allow entry level professionals to gain valuable product/industry knowledge, problem solving, and business development skills. These job opportunities enable students to begin their careers by participating in reputable professional training, sales and development programs.

Another available option is the Officer Candidates Program and Reserve Officers' Training Corps (ROTC) which was established to provide training and additional educational opportunities to gain valuable career and leadership skills. When these officers return to the private sector, employers recognize and value the discipline, technical, and operations skills they possess. Various government agencies such as the Department of Defense, Congressional Budget Office, Department of Health and Human Services, US Agency for International Development and the Center for Disease Control recruit college graduates.

Given the challenge of finding employment opportunities, even the best students will need to look at alternative opportunities as well. Look for opportunities that require the specific skills you possess. Be able to demonstrate how you acquired those skills. Talk about experiences or classes that assisted you in developing those skills. The key to success will be your ability to effectively package and sell yourself.

CHAPTER 3

Be a leader on campus.... Good grades are not enough

Leadership involvement allows you to become an integral part of your campus community and have more meaningful experiences. It gives you a voice. It is a great way to impact your campus environment and have a lasting effect. It provides great opportunities to provide solutions to problems you may have identified. Leadership involvement also enables you to develop a big picture approach to academic and social ills on your campus. It can be a great outlet for political, humanitarian, or civil rights zeal. Leadership roles will prove to be pivotal in building knowledge of the dynamics and nuances in corporations and enable you to effectively navigate their cultural and political landscapes.

Identify organizations or issues you are interested in and get involved! Quality involvement in two or three organizations is more valuable than being connected to six or seven organizations where you don't have a voice--these become an ineffective use of your time and resources. Your involvement and commitment is usually measured by the level of responsibility you assume in these organizations.

By having leadership positions, I have become more involved in different groups on campus and have been able to meet other students on a more personal level, as well as make a personal connection with the club.

3rd year Stanford student

Leadership involvement has allowed me to really see what I am capable of and better analyze my thought processes/ reactions to particular issues. Being a leader has made my college experience more interesting because I know that I've contributed to something bigger than myself and I was able to make a difference while I was in college!

4th year UGA student

Leadership involvement on my campus helped me to become a more confident and outgoing individual. When you are in a leadership position, you have to communicate information to your peers in an educated manner (sometimes even becoming a mentor for them)... Being a leader in my student organization also created many opportunities for me to network with faculty and staff within my business school, as well as with corporations.

4th year Univ. of Texas McComb student

Make sure the leadership roles you take on are beneficial to your academic and career pursuits. An obvious oversight students often make is the failure to join organizations that directly align with their major or area of interest. Interviewers expect you to demonstrate the impact you had on the organization as a result of your leadership role.

> **Example:** If you are a marketing major or an economics major with a marketing interest, you should be in the marketing, advertising or entrepreneurial club. On the other hand, if you are a finance major, taking on a PR or marketing leadership role can show evidence of creativity and well-roundedness.

> **Example:** If you are a liberal arts major, you can take on a finance/treasurer role in an organization to demonstrate your interests and improve your quantitative abilities.

If there isn't an organization on campus that addresses your interest, take the initiative and create one that allows you to pursue your passion. Identify the need and fill it! This is sure to impress employers.

Taking on leadership roles is vital to your success. We would like to add a note of caution here: Too much of anything is not necessarily a good thing. Do not get carried away with being a campus crusader and lose sight of the discipline and balance that are necessary for success. Even after you have taken on a leadership role, if you find that it is detrimental to your physical, mental and academic success, be mature and bow out gracefully. Always note that your help may be valuable, but the organization will continue whether or not you are involved.

> **Example:** A student from a college preparatory high school scored exceptionally well on SAT's, had a high school 3.9 GPA and enrolled in a top academic university. She was a leader in high school and in her community. Upon arrival on the college campus she got involved in multiple organizations and held leadership positions, but had subpar academic performance. Her 2.8 GPA compromised her ability to compete for internships and prevented her from being admitted into a select development program. She was viewed as being actively involved on her campus, yet someone who was overcommitted and unable to find the right balance of leadership and academic performance.

Time management, balancing classes, and extracurricular activities are areas where students typically struggle in their first two years on campus. If you are unsure how to strike the balance, find other student leaders or upperclassmen on campus that can help you develop a system for balancing leadership roles and academic performance. Employers look for students who are able to talk about the impact they have had in taking on leadership roles, maintaining academic excellence, and preserving a sense of self.

I had trouble balancing my school life and social life. I reached out to my family and people within my student-sponsored organization who could offer me assistance.

4th year Temple Univ. student

I would encourage them to form bonds with upperclassmen who know the rules of the "game" of their respective colleges. Furthermore, I would encourage them to never be afraid to ask for help and to use every relevant resource.

3rd year Northwestern Univ. student

Student-athletes are inherently thought of as leaders. Athletes can utilize their team involvement to demonstrate that they are leaders on campus. Remember, athletes should take advantage of their access and exposure to administrators, student body, local media and alumni. Often their schedules prevent club or organizational involvement; therefore, they must know how to highlight the discipline, time management, teamwork, sacrifice and social skills required to be a successful student-athlete.

Being a leader on campus also provides increased exposure to professors, administrators, community leaders and recruiters. You will be positioned to obtain much-needed recommendations for internships, leadership programs, fellowships, and graduate or law school.

Involvement in student organizations provides the unique opportunity to form relationships with a broad segment of your campus population. These relationships can prove vital in developing and realizing your professional goals. One note of caution, when deciding on organizations to join, you should get involved in organizations that stretch beyond your ethnicity. Employers look for students who can work across cultural divides. When reviewing your resume, if you are only involved with groups that you ethnically identify with, interviewers may interpret it as an inability or unwillingness to adapt.

It is important that you develop a leadership style that will work on your campus and help you transition into the workplace. Employers require leadership. They look for candidates who have taken on leadership roles and are able to provide evidence of their ability to work on teams, solve problems, delegate responsibility, exhibit creativity and demonstrate quantitative skills.

Leadership roles in organizations are great complements and often can be viewed as good substitutes when you lack internship experiences. Employers use leadership experiences to specifically assess your ability to:

- Meet deadlines

- Be effective under pressure

- Overcome obstacles and setbacks

- Make effective presentations

- Set priorities

- Resolve conflict

- Collaborate with others

- Balance competing demands

- Initiate change to enhance productivity

- Communicate ideas to groups

- Analyze data

- Influence the work of peers

- Manage budgets

Whether you choose to pursue a career in the family business, nonprofit sector, corporations, or academia, you will draw on the skills and exposure you gain as a leader on campus.

CHAPTER 4

Build Strong Relationships

Transitioning to a new environment on your college campus can be intimidating and daunting. Contact upperclassmen and reach out to friends or relatives that may know students on your new campus. It is important to establish a network of peers that you trust and with whom you can be honest and have no fear of being unfairly judged. Begin creating a personal community of individuals with whom you will enjoy eating meals, watching movies or simply spending time. Establish routines and customs with these new friends. Be creative. Something as simple forming a birthday club or organizing first Friday film nights with your dorm residents can be fun. The goal is to have personal interactions and form connections. Greeting other students every morning with "hello" can help you establish yourself as a friendly and likeable person. Creating your own community of peers and professors/administrators will reduce home sickness and loneliness, and add an element of excitement and expectancy to your new surroundings.

College presents a unique opportunity to invent or reinvent yourself. You should not leave your college campus having only attended your college or having just taken classes there. You should take advantage of the access and exposure a college setting provides. Commit to opening up your world to new experiences and people that you would otherwise not have had exposure to or encountered. Your new world should consist of individuals of different social, economic, racial, ethnic and even geographic backgrounds.

Getting accustomed to a new environment with new people was challenging. My college is very unlike my hometown, so the adjustment was quite big - though it was more of an issue my freshman year.

4th year Georgetown student

At all costs, avoid the common mistake of following the path of least resistance. Look for opportunities to add diversity to your college experience. Do not segregate yourself into a world on campus that only consists of people you are most familiar with or who are already like you. This choice will severely limit your ability to grow. The people you meet in college can become your network for life. If you can step out of your comfort zone and acquire these socialization skills, you will find your transition into the workplace to be a smoother and more enjoyable process.

To achieve this balance and have what will prove to be a rewarding experience, you must begin initiating and cultivating relationships.

Cultivate important relationships with:

- Classmates

- Professors/administrators

- Alumni

- Mentors

- Organizations (Church, fraternities, sororities)

- Family

- Community leaders

Friends/Classmates

"Make" friends with classmates. One important aspect of your first year is the opportunity to make new friendships. The word "make" is an active verb. That is, sitting back and waiting for friendships to happen is not an effective strategy. You must take the lead and play an active role in "making" friendships happen by starting conversations, issuing invitations, joining clubs, and organizing events. Extend yourselves and push beyond your comfort zone. If you have been shy in the past, this is a great opportunity to re-invent yourself as an outgoing individual.

Example: A third year transfer student faced having to fit in on a new campus. She was assigned to live in a freshman dorm and didn't know anyone on campus. The first person she met was a young man who offered to help carry her trunk up three flights of stairs. He immediately introduced her to others in his dorm, and his fraternity brothers became her big brothers. From day one, she made a concerted effort to connect with others, starting with dorm peers, classmates, teammates and others who had similar schedules and interests. Interestingly enough, many of those individuals remain her closest friends. She had a positive and successful experience because she took a proactive role in working to connect with others.

Choose your friends because you enjoy their company and because of their values, not because they are rich, popular and well connected. The true value of the relationship will be a byproduct of your ability to connect beyond the superficial layer and maintain those relationships beyond your college years.

College has been an enormous part in the expansion of my character and knowledge. It has opened me up to new areas and given me a chance to meet and interact with environments and people I otherwise would not have.

4th year Georgetown student

This is not to say that you can't be strategic in identifying relationships to pursue. In fact, you should be intentional in aligning yourself with individuals who can fulfill a specific purpose. It's perfectly acceptable to seek out others who may have strengths, knowledge, or experience in areas that you don't. One way to accomplish this is study groups. Getting involved in study groups is essential to your college success. This increases your understanding of the material and your efficiency in completing assignments. These are the individuals you will come to depend upon. It allows you to showcase your strengths and for others to benefit. Study groups are great incubators for forming relationships with your classmates but be prepared to actively contribute to the group effort.

There is a study group that my peers and I have formed and we get together the week before [an exam] and throughout the week to study together. We do a lot of studying by ourselves and come together to get certain things explained or do a Jeopardy type of study, where someone tests us on different problems/definitions.

3rd year Univ. of Illinois student

Freshman year they took a lot of time but none that I thought impacted my grades directly. Now in my 3rd year, there is a correlation.

3rd year Cornell Univ. student

Even though I have decent grades, I could have potentially done better. I definitely recommend finding a group of FOCUSED AND HARD WORKING individuals to work with in a disciplined way. I did not use study groups. This is a big regret. My college career was much more difficult due to this mistake.

4ᵗʰ year Kennesaw State student

Professors/Administrators

A natural way to initiate relationships with professors is taking advantage of their office hours. Often material that is difficult to understand in class may be easily mastered in a one-on-one setting. In addition, visiting with professors and teaching assistants can reveal other available resources, special projects, internships, scholarships, and development programs. Your professors are often industry experts and typically have valuable industry networks. This strategy only works if you consistently attend the professor's class and arrive on time.

I have never used a tutor. I try to push myself to go to my professor's office hours. This has helped me build relationships with some of them and it helped my grades in instances where I needed the help.

3ʳᵈ year Florida State Univ. student

It is always situation dependent. Sometimes you get lucky and have a great professor/TA and they are very helpful. Other times they are a waste of your time. The key is you have to try before you know, so it is good to go to office hour at least once early in every course you take...I used TA/professor office hours consistently, especially in my econ class. The result is never getting below a B in my econ classes.

3rd year Univ. of Chicago student

I usually try to pick the professors who are the most distinguished in their respective fields. For me, it was really helpful to be in a class with a particular professor who was always in the news. All universities have their star professors that students should seek out and take their courses.

4th year NYU student

Even when you are performing very well in a class, it is still important to utilize office hours to build a relationship with your professor. This creates a great platform to secure impactful letters of recommendation and internships.

Office hours are very important, as they help in building relationships with your professors. I like to discuss the materials that are being taught in class because they usually interest me. This also helps the professor know that you have studied the material thoroughly.

3rd year Dartmouth student

I wish I had known it was possible to get a 3.7 or above in my first semester. I had in mind that it was near impossible to do that, when in fact I see students around me getting grades in that range. I would advise that each student go to office hours!! It is unbelievable how critical this is!

3rd year Columbia student

Alumni

Initiate relationships with alumni who can serve as mentors and industry experts. They should be called upon to gain industry insight and provide access to career opportunities that may not be available via normal channels. When contacting alumni, you must remember that they are professionals. Be respectful of their time, position and ability to influence. A misstep here can cost you a career with their organizations and can negatively impact your reputation on campus. Do your home-work and research prior to initiating contact with them.

Organizations

Joining a sorority or fraternity is a personal choice. These organiza-tions can facilitate a sense of belonging on your college campus and pre-vent isolation. Fraternities and sororities provide exceptional lifelong friendships and networking opportunities. Yet timing is critical. Plan ahead! Structure a course load that will accommodate pledging require-ments. Failure to do so can negatively impact your GPA and relation-ships with professors.

Pledging, although extremely time consuming, did not really affect my grades. I would have to say it took a toll on my line brothers though, decreasing their GPA's to the lowest of all semesters.

3rd year Baruch College student

I pledged during the fall semester of my junior year. It did not affect my GPA; I actually made the dean's list. My GPA went up.

4th year Cornell student

I pledged during my freshman year and I wish I would have waited. Being in a fraternity takes a lot of involvement in extracurricular activities which I feel have had a minimal but still noticeable effect on my GPA.

4th year Univ. of Oklahoma student

At first, I think it was rough for me to learn how to properly balance my social life in a fraternity with my school work. My GPA probably dropped by almost half a point because of it. By mid-sophomore year, however, I was able to figure out the correct balance and raise my grades. However, if I could go back in time to pledge in a different year, I still wouldn't because of the invaluable lessons I learned.

4th year MIT student

Family/Community

Maintain relationships with family and community leaders. These connections represent opportunities to develop valuable support systems and mentorships. They offer a much-needed adult perspective now that your parents are less involved in your daily interactions and decision making. It can provide balance to the implied expertise of your 18-20 year old roommates and peers. Getting involved in community organizations also gives you an opportunity to take on leadership roles and advance causes that you are passionate about; it is a great way to give back. It is a great asset on your resume. These involvements help you remember or realize it's not always just about you.

Religious organizations and local places of worship represent a great opportunity to gain spiritual fulfillment and create surrogate families while away from home.

Create a Network

In addition to the relationships you've established on your campus and with the community, you should also have "go-to" individuals. These will be people that you can immediately turn or run to when you need help. Here are few situations for you to consider and begin to think about who you would "go to" should you face any of these dilemmas:

- Have an emergency and you need money right now

- Get in legal trouble or arrested

- Get sick or have medical concerns

- Have roommate issues

- Failing a class

- Suffering emotionally/mentally

- Overwhelmed

In your network, you should have individuals already in place or begin to identify those who can address the needs identified above. Transparency and honesty are critical in obtaining help and resolving situations.

> **Example:** A first generation, third year college student became overwhelmed with working to help cover tuition, maintaining academic performance, and difficulties back home. When she realized she couldn't manage all these competing demands, she withdrew from school six weeks into the semester. She went home and looked for a job to earn money. Note: this happens time and time again and not just to first generation college students.

Lacking the right go-to people, she made her decision without any input from others. The individuals in a position to help did not become aware of her challenges until after she dropped out of school for that semester. As a first generation college student, she didn't have the parental and family support to make it through this difficult period. Having made all of her college enrollment and financial aid decisions on her own, she wasn't aware of the support system that was readily available to her. That support system included career counselors, financial aid representatives, professors, academic advisors, mentors, friends and their resources.

Had she reached out to any of the above individuals at the first sign of trouble, a plan could have been put in place that would have enabled her to stay in school.

Your network should include individuals who:

- will tell you the truth and make you aware of resulting consequences

- have wisdom and resources

- can connect you with the appropriate experts

- know when you are not being forthright and truthful and will call you on it

- will encourage and inspire you

You have to develop and maintain authentic relationships with other adults where you feel safe and can have open and honest dialogue about issues that are important to you. These adults should have the ability to be nonjudgmental, yet offer the wisdom and concern you need. One of the greatest challenges you will face is knowing when and how to ask for help. You must have individuals in your life that will help you make balanced choices. Be teachable, open to new ideas, and alternative solutions!

> **Example:** A student attended a prominent, liberal arts college. After completing her second year, she decided to transfer to another college. The new college offered a specific major in the retail industry, the area where she wanted to begin her career. Upon learning of her decision (she had already completed the transfer), mentors and advisors shared with her that if she focused on the intrinsic value of a liberal arts education, the reputation of her school and its alumni power; she would realize that she was not making a well informed decision. She was put in touch with successful retail industry professionals that were alumni of her liberal arts college.

She responded swiftly. She pursued the contacts provided, performed the additional research suggested and investigated the placement statistics of the new school. She was able to recognize that her 3.6 GPA, industry interest and preparation, and reputation of her liberal arts college would position her to obtain the job opportunities she desired without that specific retail major.

After a semester, she transferred back to her liberal arts school (she remained in contact with them) and secured an internship with a prestigious organization in the retail industry. She was very fortunate that she had adults and advisors in her life that were able to provide better information. She *listened* and was able to recognize advice that worked in her present and future "best" interest and *acted* on that information. As she moves into her senior year of college, she may decide on a different career path. Her liberal arts college, the scope of her classes (economics, finance, psychology), her strong GPA, and the strength of her career services office position her to take advantage of many different career options.

I highly regret never establishing a relationship with someone to mentor me who I admired or valued enough to imitate and seek council from. I was never as mentor-seeking as I would have liked nor humble enough to ask.

4th year Georgetown student

I had a rough semester due to personal situations at home and a load of stuff going on at school and all. I ended up not doing well in my classes that semester because of it. I had never run into a problem with bad grades so I didn't know how to handle the situation. A few people that I knew helped me figure things out and I went to my dean, who helped me work things out for that semester.

3rd year Florida State Univ. student

Example: A third year college student with exceptional academic and leadership involvement on campus and in the community reached a point where everything began to unravel. An unresolved personal experience caused her emotional and mental distress. Her grades suffered and she withdrew from leadership activities and began to make very poor career and personal decisions. She knew she needed help, but being a high achiever and trying to manage the high expectations of her family and mentors, she held it all in and plowed forward, believing that it would work itself out. She subsequently failed a class.

She finally began to seek help. Her school administrators, academic advisors and mentors were eager to help her when they became aware of the magnitude of her situation. They were willing to offer assistance because of her reputation on campus, previous academic performance, and campus involvement. She was allowed to take appropriate steps that would enable her to recover; however, she could have avoided the mental stress and embarrassment of this situation had she sought help earlier.

There is an old saying, "At the first sign of smoke, yell fire!" Never be afraid to ask for advice and help. People will be willing to assist you if you have done your part.

CHAPTER 5

Understand the value of integrity

Integrity, by definition, means adhering especially to moral or artistic values; quality or state of being complete or undivided, according to Merriam Webster's Dictionary. A person of integrity has integrated his or her standards, words, and actions into one. Integrity, then, is saying what you mean, meaning what you say, doing what you say, and meaning what you do![17] A person's character is ultimately defined by integrity, and character can be defined by what you do when no one else is looking.

Honesty and integrity go hand in hand. You cannot have one without the other.

Your actions and words must be consistent. Do what you say you are going to do!

No excuses!

---

17   Dr. Jeff Iorg, "Foundations for Integrity in Leadership," June 23, 2008. Internet; accessed Dec 2009.

Integrity defines who you are; it is not situational. Lack of integrity is when a person's beliefs and actions conflict with each other or when there are gaping holes in their expressed beliefs as a result of their actions[18].

Examples:

- You state that you value time; yours and others. You agree to meet with your study group at a particular time and you arrive late.

- You tell your friends that you believe in treating everyone with respect and then refuse to speak to your roommate's guests when they visit too often.

- You believe that everyone should be treated fairly but you request a room change when you discover your new roommate is from a different racial background.

In all of the cases above, what you said you believed in was different from your actions and therefore you exhibited a lack of personal integrity.

---

18   Garry Hamilton, "A Brief Bio," 2008, Internet; accessed Dec 2009.

When I think about integrity, I think about following through on what you say you will do. I also think it means standing by what you believe, despite what people are doing around you. I think my personal integrity was an issue during my freshman year when I was trying to fit in with students I didn't really connect with. Because I was not with a group of people who validated who I was, I lost some integrity and would cave into peer pressure and act differently from how I normally would if I felt comfortable with myself and my environment.

3rd year Stanford student

I think of what a person does behind closed doors when no one is looking. I think of a person who is sympathetic and down-to-earth, because without integrity people can often be selfish and arrogant. I think of standing up for something when no one else will. I also think of having to stand alone from the crowd whenever it is necessary.

3rd year Univ. of Southern CA student

Integrity means being honest and responsible. This applies to the collegiate world by doing your own work and being able to honestly say you did this assignment/project within ethical and moral boundaries to the best of your ability.

3rd year Georgetown Univ. student

Integrity is a decision. As you begin your new life on a college campus you need to make a decision to:

- Do what's right

- Be honest; do what you say you're going to do

- Be dependable

Myth: Cheating is acceptable as long as you don't get caught.

Reality: Obtaining a test from any source other than your professor is considered cheating and can result in expulsion.

Your integrity will be challenged throughout your academic and professional career. Make the decision that your response to situations and events will not be driven by what personally benefits you versus what is the right thing to do. Remember, you are in this for the long haul. You need to protect and preserve you name... your brand. When students exercise poor judgment, it is often the result of desperately wanting something or the fear of losing something. Unfortunately, a pattern of poor judgment often results in the student being labeled as a person of questionable character.

We find it tragic when talented students who have done all the right things are unable to realize their dreams and ambitions because of poor decisions around integrity, failing to honor commitments, and the absence of simple honesty in many of their actions. We see scores of students that are bright and seem to have it all together, yet there is an area that is inconsequential to them but speaks volumes to us and is usually echoed by employers regarding concerns about their character or ability to be forthright. You will often hear this expressed as, "there is something about him/her I can't put my finger on but they are not a good fit for us". Each year, we witness students who have worked very hard to have successful college careers, miss out on amazing opportunities because they exercised poor judgment on major and at time, insignificant issues. Even innocent mistakes can prove to be costly.

> **Example:** A student accepted an offer to intern for an investment bank. The application process included detailed questions about previous arrests and/or any expunged police records. In completing the application, she indicated that she had no police record or prior incidents. Her background check revealed felony charges on her record. While working in her internship, it was brought to her attention. She explained that when she first started college, she had been arrested for using a fake ID and was charged with a misdemeanor. She defended her actions on the application because the charges were completely expunged by the court. Her intention was not to deceive. She believed her record was clean, but the questions were detailed enough for her to explain her situation and she chose not to. She was able to provide proof of the expunged record; however, the bank informed her that she would not be eligible to obtain full-time employment with them.

Integrity to me is doing the right thing when no one is looking. When I was a student at my previous school they had an honor code, as most schools do, which I tried to follow strictly. I have never really been in a situation before but I can discuss a story about my friend and his decision. He was studying for his exam and looking for review materials online and he accidentally found the actual exam. The exam was a document in the review folder with all the other materials. My roommate chose to alert the professor and another exam was given. My roommate was actually struggling in the course; however, he still had integrity.

4th year NYU student

Integrity is doing what is right even when you think no one else is watching. An easy example of a situation where integrity is involved is in the case of online quizzes/tests. The teacher is not there to monitor whether or not the student is taking the test by him/herself or not using any notes. It's up to the student to take the initiative to follow directions even when they know there's no way for the teacher to know if they cheated or not.

4th year UGA student

Example: A student applied for a very prestigious internship that required submission of the names of individuals who would provide recommendations for her. The student notified the individuals she selected. One recommender was surprised that her name had been submitted. Furthermore, this recommender had observed actions and behavior by the candidate that did not allow her to feel fully comfortable attaching her name as a recommender to this candidate. Not wanting to raise any red flags or cause embarrassment for the student, she provided a strong recommendation.

The student received the offer and that particular recommendation played a significant role in her ability to secure the internship. Several weeks went by and the recommender again witnessed behavior that led to her initial uneasiness regarding the students' ability to be consistent and dependable. The recommender shared with the student the awkward position she had been placed in having to provide a recommendation and the concern regarding the student's ability to perform well in the internship and the potential reputation damage the recommender might suffer.

The student admitted the need for improvement and changes in her behavior and also revealed that the other recommender had shared similar concerns with her.

In your attempt to secure leadership and employment opportunities, your integrity will be evaluated. When you involve others for referrals or recommendations, your behavior and reputation has the potential to impact their integrity as well. Always receive permission to use someone for a recommendation prior to submitting their name. All recommendations are not equal. If someone is uncomfortable speaking on your behalf, they may provide a recommendation, but it might not be the type of recommendation that will advance your candidacy.

Common Sense

Common sense is not so common. It is defined as an internal sense which allows for clear understanding and enables one to make good decisions.[19] It is instinctively knowing what to do without having to give thought to it or needing to seek guidance. If you don't possess common sense, you should be more observant of your environment. Take cues from those around you and seek advice or counsel from others.

> *Go with your gut, always. Don't let people convince you not to do something unless their advice is sound, and based on evidence, or some sort of personal experience. When people use personal experience as the basis for their advice; make sure you are similar in background and their advice will be more relevant to you.*

> **3rd year Stanford student**

---

19   Wikipedia. Definition of Common Sense, Internet; accessed Dec 2009.

When it comes to situations in which you aren't really sure about whether or not you should participate, listen to what your conscience tells you. If you think that the situation would be beneficial for your growth as a person, by all means take the opportunity without regret. But if you think that the bad consequences substantially outweigh the good in a given situation, do not participate in any way. No one knows what you need better than you do in those types of situations, and you have to trust yourself in order to get through whatever life throws at you.

3rd year Fisk Univ. student

I think that I consistently employ common sense and good judgment when it comes to my decisions. The impact that this has had is that I have never gotten into the kind of trouble that I know friends of mine have (DUI, for example). This has also helped me become the person that my friends always come to for advice, and I do take that as flattering.

4th year Univ. of Texas, McComb student

Simple common sense examples:

- Showing up for class five to ten minutes early

- Arriving at an interview 15-30 minutes before your scheduled start time

- Striking the appropriate balance between studying and partying, (e.g. not going out the night before an exam)

- Knowing where to go for your interview

- Returning the overage when the cashier gives you too much change

- Holding the door open for the person behind you

Judgment

Good judgment is being accountable for your actions. Saying just enough to get what you want is not being truthful.   Straightforward and clear communication will establish credibility and build trust. When you make a mistake be quick to offer a sincere apology.

> **Example:** You have multiple job offers and varying deadlines. You have decided on the offer you are go-ing to accept. After you accept your offer, you should immediately notify the other companies that you are declining their offer. This is a professional courtesy you should adhere to, even though the deadline for the other offers has not been reached.

Example: You are struggling in a class. Do not wait until the week of finals to visit the professor/TA to ask for help.

Good judgment is such an important attribute that it is often listed first on an employer's list of qualities required of job applicants. Judgment is defined as the capacity to assess situations or circumstances and draw sound conclusions.

CHAPTER 6

Build a powerful brand….."Brand You"

A brand is an identification mark, a trade name given to a product or service.

It is what you come to depend on, consistency, a promise--your reputation…built on prior performance.

Here are examples of some well known brands. They clearly communicate the brand's promise and reputation.

Apple	BMW
Coca Cola	Disney
Gatorade	Google
Microsoft	Nike
Pepsi	Sony
IBM	Sprite

Creating Your "Brand You!"

You are responsible for creating your own personal brand. If you are not intentional in creating and defining "who" you are, your brand--others will automatically brand you positively or negatively based on observed behaviors, actions, and impressions.

In developing your brand, here is a list of action words that you can use to describe yourself:

PROACTIVE	HARDWORKING
PRACTICAL	RESOURCEFUL
CONSISTENT	DEPENDABLE
TRUSTWORTHY	THOROUGH
INNOVATIVE	PREPARED
CREATIVE	IMAGINATIVE
HAPPY	FRIENDLY
DILIGENT	METICULOUS
INVENTIVE	POSITIVE
RELIABLE	PRODUCTIVE
UNFAILING	DILIGENT

Before you can create a winning brand, you must conduct an assessment of:

1. How you define yourself
2. How others (peers, professors, family) perceive you
3. How you want to be perceived
4. Reconciling the inconsistencies in the perception of who you are

The next step in creating a winning personal brand is to:

1. Have a clear understanding of your strengths and weaknesses
2. Know how to accentuate your strengths
3. Be deliberate in minimizing weaknesses. This requires honesty and action
4. Choose five action words that you want attached to your brand and find opportunities and involvements that will allow others to use those words to define you

The inability to be reflective and honest about your shortcomings usually results in having a personal perspective of your brand that differs from how others perceive you. You should ask friends, family and professors to describe who they perceive you to be and compare that to who you perceive yourself to be. Get feedback from those individuals to address any inconsistencies or disconnects. Identify specific changes in behavior, attitudes, actions and personal traits that will enable you address these voids.

Your brand identity will be a blend of traits and characteristics that are unique to your particular brand ("Brand You") and what the marketplace values. You can create an air of approachability and openness through something as simple as a smile. Many social or professional opportunities will pass you by if you have an air of unfriendliness. It's not just wearing a smile on your face. It goes deeper. It's having a genuine concern and interest in others and the ability to convey that you are a happy and confident person. The identity of your brand involves every aspect of who you are.

Your brand is defined by:

- Knowledge and preparation

- Oral Communication skills (use of informal language/slang, accents)

- Written communication (grammar, fluency)

- Interactions with others (formal, informal)

- Friends and associations (fraternities, sororities, athletics, campus organizations)

- Etiquette (attire and manners)

Example: A student had a strong academic record (4.0 GPA) at a competitive state college, great interpersonal and writing skills, was a strong leader on campus and very engaging, with excellent follow through interviewed for an internship. She scored well on the company's assessment test. She was offered the opportunity. As she took time to determine if this was the right company and position, the recruiter who was eager to have her work for his company offered her additional internship options not available to other candidates. In the end, the power of her brand resulted in the company offering her the ability to create and structure an internship to fit her specific needs and interests in hopes of securing her candidacy.

A positive brand reputation impacts the effectiveness of your leadership on campus. This will give you the opportunity to participate in different leadership activities; it affords you support from administrators and professors; and it earns you the respect of your peers. Your brand should be strong enough to withstand a mistake or misstep. The strength of your brand should enable others to give you a second chance.

Here are some responses we received from our research when we asked students how they created their brand:

My personal brand is just a more refined version of who I've always been. I identified parts of my personality that I needed to work on, and I've worked on them. Some traits of my brand are: hardworking, enthusiastic, analytical, a team player. By having a consistent brand, other students know that I'm a good person to partner with on projects, and employers know that I will get the job done and be excited about it along the way.

4th year MIT student

I identified what I was good at and what I had been involved in on campus and tailored it to fit what job I wanted or was looking for.

4th year Univ. of Georgia student

I created my "personal brand" by listing the four traits about me that I felt I brought to any given situation. Those traits are: 1. Eagerness to learn and be useful to the project; 2. Punctuality in completing assignments or being at a place at the time requested; 3. Creative approaches to solving problems and the ability to make them relate to multiple demographics; 4. Integrity and honesty when it comes to the degree of my failures and successes. My personal brand has led me to many successful ventures, both in school and out of school.

3rd year Fisk Univ. student

By focusing on how I wanted others to see me. Truthfulness, competitiveness, and hardworking are traits of my personal brand. They have helped me succeed in college because I have had to work hard for my grades but earn them in an honest way.

4th year Stanford student

When I think of a personal brand, I really think about just being comfortable in my own skin and confident in my abilities. It's also important to realize that everyone you meet, you are not going to connect with or get along well with. This is natural and I think it's important not to get frustrated by it. That was something that took me some time to realize. Once I realized that was okay, I was able to relax and be more comfortable when I was talking to someone.

4th year NYU student

Once you create your brand, you must be vigilant in protecting it. Guard against behavior that can taint your brand. Clear, open and honest communication will help you avoid compromising situations. Value your word and honor all responsibilities and obligations. If circumstances arise that prohibit you from doing what you have committed to do, inform the appropriate people of new developments. Never be a no-show.

Students often fall in the trap of using excuses to explain or justify behavior and performance. Here are a few excuses that have been given by students when they failed to meet deadlines for submitting assignments:

I apologize, I sent it last week but I just saw where it did not go through.

I sent my resume to you this past weekend. But since I was in another city, the connection might not have worked well enough for you to receive it.

I apologize for the delay. Things have been particularly rough lately.

I sincerely apologize about getting this to you so late. I had to baby sit today and the internet in their home was not working.

An all time favorite is:

I have been extremely busy and have not had adequate time to devote to revising my resume. However, do you have any suggestions as to how I might improve the resume?

Excuses as a ready defense for your shortcomings is a sure way to damage your brand. Be a person of integrity and do what you commit to do. When you fail or make a mistake, admit the misstep and move on.

Remember, Facebook, voicemail, Twitter, and other social media vehicles will positively or negatively impact your brand. You must be careful to use these vehicles in a manner that is consistent with the brand you have created. Employers use these media vehicles as reference points in the hiring process. Be careful! Privacy is null and void when you put information on Twitter, Facebook, My Space, or any other virtual media vehicle. You are in effect saying to recruiters, admissions committees, scholarship review boards… This is who I am.

Common mistakes to avoid:

Voicemail: Having music as a part of your message; use of slang or unprofessional language; using someone else's voice on your message. Always answer the phone in a clear and professional manner, especially during recruiting season.

Facebook: Pictures that are inappropriate (e.g., Tequila shots at the bar, physically revealing photos, questionable group shots).

Email Addresses: Use of inappropriate email addresses (e.g., sexygirl@gmail.com, falconsfan@hotmail.com, smartiepants@yahoo.com)

> **Example:** A student received a call and answered the phone by saying, "Hey girl—what's up?" When she realized it was a recruiter from her dream company, she was embarrassed and could not recover quickly enough to effectively sell herself during the conversation. Unfortunately, based on that interaction, the recruiter made the decision not to pursue her as a candidate for that opportunity.

Review the list below of individuals that have created winning personal brands.

Albert Einstein	Barack Obama
Beyonce'	Bill Gates
Denzel Washington	Dr. Martin Luther King Jr.
Jennifer Lopez	Jay Leno
Lance Armstrong	Michael Jackson
Michael Jordan	Oprah Winfrey
Colin Powell	Tom Cruise
Warren Buffett	Will Smith

In creating your personal brand, be true to the things that make you who you are. Improve upon the gifts and talents you have been given and create opportunities to improve upon your weaknesses/ deficiencies. Start developing a professional and polished look that will enable you to confidently become an effective campus leader and secure challenging internship opportunities.

CHAPTER 7

Choose a Career Path—your major matters but should not be a roadblock

Usually the decision to attend college is driven by the need/ desire to secure a great job or gain entry into graduate school (e.g., law, medical or business school).   While you are in college, it is critical that you obtain internships. Your pursuit of relevant internships should begin in your freshman year.   Internships are designed to give you access, exposure and experience into possible career choices.   These experiences will confirm that you have made a good selection or create awareness of your need to pursue an alternative choice.

Because I was a finance major in High School and was a part of the nationwide Academy of Finance I have been able to do career related internships since junior year in high school. So I have had five summers' worth of internships. This impacted my ability tremendously because my last internship transitioned into a full-time offer.

4th year Univ. of Buffalo student

Use your summer wisely with internships or fellowship opportunities, beginning freshman year. Start planning for summers in December.

4th year Yale Univ. student

Selecting a Major

Let's take a step back and talk about your major. You must consider the following:

1) Why did you decide on this major?

2) Are you genuinely interested in the subject matter of your major?

3) Are you performing well in your major?

4) For your chosen major, what is the typical career path?

5) Does your major provide you with the necessary skills for your career interests and/or the ability to be employed in a position worthy of a college degree?

Students often mistakenly believe that having a double major and a minor is impressive and will differentiate them from the competition. We suggest that you simplify your academic life and reduce stress levels by selecting one major in an area that you are most interested or an area that aligns with your career aspirations and be committed to that area of study. By avoiding the double major route of congestion: you free yourself to take more of the classes you want; increase your ability to participate in study abroad or other special interest programs; and increase the odds of graduating on time. You will also gain the freedom to experiment with classes where you have a natural curiosity. Double majors equate to double the work but not necessarily double the return on the investment. A single major will give you room in your academic curriculum to take specific classes that will permit you to develop exposure or expertise. Performing well in any given major will allow you to be more competitive than students with double majors whose GPA is average at best. Interviewers are likely to pay attention to the major you have listed first, particularly when it's in line with the job opportunities you are pursuing.

Look at your course catalog and choose a major based on the likability of most of the classes you would have to take and positive experiences other students have had with the professors in that major. Create a set up for success. Getting through the prerequisites is a major barrier for some. Combine some "fun" classes with the challenging required courses to make your experience more enjoyable.

Some students are very fortunate in that they know without a doubt what they want to do. Others have a pretty good idea and need to narrow their focus and decide between majors. Then there are others who have no concrete idea of their interests, yet they believe they know what they do not want to do.

I chose to be a marketing major because I found it to be an exciting path of study. I originally wanted to become a finance guru since it promised me wealth, but I was not aware of what the field demanded from an individual. I took a course and found that my interest did not lie there. Marketing, on the other hand, is something I can relate to. I love to study consumers and love the ongoing efforts of attracting customers through various and endless channel possibilities.

3rd year Baruch College student

I chose my major because sociology has always been something that has interested me. I attend a liberal arts university, therefore we don't have specialized majors like business. I was able to major in sociology but also took classes across many different disciplines. My major doesn't directly support my career aspirations but there are definitely transferable skills that will help me in my future career. For example, learning about sociology will aid me in a marketing career and better allow me to understand the customer.

4th year Connecticut College student

I chose political science because I like law, politics, public speaking, thinking & reasoning, reading and writing, and blending different disciplines together in order to study the issues of power and justice. In my mind the three power pillars of the world are money, religion and law, and political science afforded me the opportunity to examine all three of them broadly.

3rd year Fisk University student

I chose my major and redirected my focus from finance because I realized that it didn't interest me as much I as had thought. Also, my first internship allowed me to realize this as well. My current major of accounting is in line with my career aspirations of becoming a CPA and maybe in the long term becoming the CFO of a company.

3rd year Florida State Univ. student

Choosing a Career

Visit your career services office and speak with counselors or go online and take a Career Assessment Test (e.g. Career Leader, Careerfitter.com, CareerMaze, Career Interest Survey). If you are uncertain, it will help you identify potential career paths that align with your strengths and interests. If you already know what you want to do, it will substantiate your fit.

In identifying a career path, here is a great exercise you should complete:

- Identify a particular industry or arena.

- What do you envision your day to be like when you secure/land this opportunity?

- What are you doing when you arrive at work?

- What does the environment look and feel like?

- How are you dressed?

- Go as far as identifying how you will get to work and if driving, what kind of car you see yourself in.

Now that you have identified the big picture, remove the label and focus on the job content:

- What tasks are involved?

- Are you marketing, performing research, selling, creating, or collaborating?

- Are you on a team, making presentations or writing proposals?

- Does it involve projects, require organizational skills?

- Are you good at what you have identified?

You should be able to see that what you want to do isn't tied to any one position or opportunity and that you can find a fit in a host of different industries. Regardless of your major, with adequate preparation and planning, you can embark on any career path you desire (the path is much smoother if you have performed well academically). The operative word is **PREPAREDNESS**. When **OPPORTUNITY** comes, and it surely will, you should be able to convince a recruiter or hiring manager that you are the right person for the position.

You do not need to major in economics to work on Wall Street, period. Look up the work you will be doing in your classes before school starts and try to get a head start on the reading. Reach out to alumni as soon as you have decided what career fields you are interested and start shadowing professionals. Take a language, but do not overload your coursework. Getting over a 3.3 cumulative GPA is absolutely crucial to future success. NETWORK!

3rd year Amherst College student

Steps to Securing a Job

The most important piece is not your major, but that you are truly college educated. Employers are looking for students who possess leadership, analytical, and strong communication skills. You must also be well–rounded, displaying a balance between academic excellence, an ability to work with others, and a willingness to "work hard." You are not in the season of life to worry about work-life balance. Right now you should solely focus on the work part of that equation.

To secure a job opportunity you will be required to:

- Present who you are with credibility (90 second pitch). Most interviews will start with "tell me about yourself". Your response should be a synopsis about you that can include your major, campus activities, efficient highlights of work experience, and reason for pursuing the position. You should invest time developing and getting comfortable with your pitch. It will allow you to naturally talk about yourself with confidence in any given situation.

- Create an error free resume and cover letter that sells YOU. Your resume should include bulleted impact statements of your accomplishments. If you can quantify (e.g. 20% increase in sales) your results, this will enhance your resume tremendously. Cover letters are meant to give the reader a clear sense of who you are, why you are interested in the opportunity, and what you have to offer as a candidate. They should be written in such a way that they are interesting and result in the reader wanting to interview you.

- Conduct industry and company specific research utilizing vault guides, career services, press releases, annual reports and the internet.

- Talk to individuals in the industry and specific company. Develop a "target" list of companies you will pursue. Attend campus presentations, coffee chats and other company sponsored events to learn about these companies and the professionals they employ. Conduct informational interviews to ask questions about the company, its culture and the specific position of interest. Create a system or spread sheet to track all points of communication you have had with those companies. Schedule mock interviews with friends, professionals and your career services center.

- Interviewing is an art. It requires preparation and above all practice, practice, practice. Prepare using the same approach you would take with exams. Diligence pays off! After you have developed a system that is effective, you will use it again and again for all subsequent interviews. Review the job description and specific job responsibilities. Prepare questions to ask during your interview.

- Prepare your responses to interview questions in advance of the interview. Write them out. Rehearse in front of a mirror. Record your responses and review your performance; listen with a critical ear to focus on individual areas that need improvement. Most interviews are behavioral based. This requires story telling ability, salesmanship and great command of details and outcomes. Interviewers will rely on previous behavior as a predictor of future performance.

- Sell/market "Brand You" in a way that is relevant to the company you are interviewing with. Match your skills/ talents and experiences to the specific position. Interviewers expect you to demonstrate how your leadership positions and previous work experience enabled you to have an impact. You will need to further communicate how those experiences are relevant to the company and the specific position to which you are applying.

- Use the STAR system when answering questions. This structured method of answering questions will enable you to provide answers in an orderly and efficient manner. It gives you a clear beginning and end. You will describe the **situation,** the **task** that needed to be accomplished, the **action** you took and the **results** of your actions. Use this system to demonstrate that you are a problem solver. Be poised, relaxed and confident.

- Make eye contact and have a firm hand shake. If you are uncomfortable looking someone straight in the eyes, focus on another facial feature. The nose is a good substitute. Avoid staring. It can make the interviewer uncomfortable. It is completely acceptable to take notes in an interview. Maintain eye contact even while taking notes. We recommend a spiral notebook or portfolio with an attached notepad to prevent papers from getting shuffled or falling to the floor. Be aware of the interviewer's body language. Body language can help you detect boredom, interest, answers that are too long, and responses that were confusing. These nonverbal cues should help you make appropriate adjustments during the interview.

- At the end of the interview, have three to four well researched questions to ask that demonstrate your understanding of the position, company and shows intellectual curiosity. The best questions to ask are ones in which you are truly interested in the answers.

- Conduct appropriate follow-up. Always send a thank you note. It is an opportunity to express your appreciation for the interviewer's time and interest in your candidacy. It also gives you another chance to sell yourself, add clarity to points you made during the interview, and to reiterate why you should be hired for the position.

Select a major, choose a career path and secure internships that will allow you to begin your professional career in a position that brings fulfillment and reward.

STUDENT SUCCESS STORIES

Three former students share their amazing and thought provoking personal stories of how they successfully navigated the college years, secured internships and graduated at the top of their classes. They have positions in very challenging and competitive industries: management consulting, brand management and oil and energy. We trust you will find these stories inspiring and informative.

I chose my college based mainly on its academic rigor. My biggest thing when choosing a school was making sure that I was positioning myself in an environment that was very similar to what I would see in corporate America. Something else I liked about my choice was the urban campus environment. It also helped to have the Hope Scholarship (a merit scholarship provided by the state for residents who attend in-state colleges or universities). I didn't want to go into debt for an undergraduate degree, so I chose a school in state where funding was provided to make sure that was possible.

Lastly, I liked that my college presented opportunities for me to challenge myself. The campus was big enough where I would have to do big things and forge relationships across the entire campus to leave an indelible mark.

In selecting classes, time management was key. I set a schedule that I could get comfortable with. In determining my schedule, I made sure to prioritize the things that mattered most, but also left time for me to do things that would keep me sane while in school. For example, getting time in the gym was something that was important to me. I made sure that I made time for the gym as if it were one of my scheduled classes. I disciplined myself to do it as a part of my schedule instead of struggling with the frustration of trying to fit it into my schedule when things got hectic. In terms of selecting classes, I made sure that I didn't take too many math/quant heavy courses all in the same semester, even though I was good at math. I tried my best to have balance. Although I ALWAYS strived for A's, if for whatever reason there were certain classes that turned out to be difficult, I'd have other classes to help me keep a sustainable GPA.

I found it important to introduce myself to all my teachers at the beginning of every semester. The focus here was making sure that professors knew more than just a name, but my face as well. As far as office hours were concerned, I used them whenever I felt it w[as] necessary, most specifically in preparation for tests that I thought would be difficult and/or to discuss the things I got wrong on tests/exams when I got them back. I strategically leveraged all resources on campus, professors being included, to my advantage. With my professors, I didn't want to wait until the end of the semester to forge a relationship when I needed to discuss my grade. I wanted them to know I was present, committed, and vested in my performance in their classroom.

I didn't really find much benefit in study groups because most of the time, I felt like I was expected to lead them, which wasn't always helpful for me. At times, however, I did find that teaching other people how to do certain things helped me to better reinforce my own learning of the material. My campus schedule was really hectic, so most times study groups weren't convenient.

I also sought insight from advisors, professors, and other students when choosing courses. There were resources on campus to let us know the average GPA in certain courses, by professor, so that we would know what to expect from a particular professor teaching the class. Those items were key in my schedule making.

I created a budget. The budget was broken into essentials, near-essentials, and non-essentials. The essentials were food, gas, tithes, and any bills. Part of the food budget was figuring out how many days a week I needed to eat out vs. cooking. Near-essentials were items like hair, nails, etc. Non-essentials were shopping and other forms of entertainment. If nothing else, I stuck with the budget I created for myself and kept a record for budget vs. actual spent in each category as a basis for making the budget for the next month.

In choosing campus leadership positions, I chose positions that would allow me to gain certain skills that were relevant to [my] career interests. For example, because I was studying finance, I sought a position as treasurer in an organization as opposed to the role of president. I also chose to be involved in positions and organizations that I could be committed to and show involvement over the course of my entire college experience, somewhere I could get involved and stay. Building credibility is hard when you're involved in a bunch of different organizations each year. I wanted to build and maintain credibility so that I could do as many different positions that I was interested in one or two organizations that I liked as opposed to one position in several different organizations.

In identifying a career, my biggest advice is to write down the items that are important to you in a job and then find a job that fits you, as opposed to fitting yourself to[a] job description. It's assessing your gifts, your strengths, and your weaknesses and deciding how to best mesh them into a job for you. The answer is figuring out what you're passionate about, deciding what work environment fits you (at a desk, being hands on, client facing, etc), how you work best (individually or in teams), and finding positions that you would enjoy. Most people take this process in reverse and fail to find job satisfaction.

2009 Georgia Tech Graduate (3.9 GPA),
Management Consultant

Growing up in a single parent home in Nashville, TN, I attended public and poorly funded schools. In the 8th grade, a teacher recommended a private, all-girls' school that I attended. I had a wonderful high school experience and did very well (that is, with a lot of very, very hard work to catch up to my peers).

 I chose Spelman College, a liberal arts college. I knew I wanted to pursue a career in business but did not know what area. I took classes in a variety of business disciplines that helped me better define my goals. Spelman was also close enough to drive home when in need of seeing my family and vice versa.

A couple of factors helped me manage my money: 1) some of the grants I received weren't reoccurring - I needed to save in case I didn't get [them] the next semester or year; 2) saving for a rainy day - you never know what emergencies are going to pop up requiring cash (or maybe it's a spring break trip or pledging a sorority/fraternity), 3) realizing that I still needed to live within my means - I didn't blow all of my money shopping.

I had a good advisor in the Economics and Honors department. I consulted my advisors about classes before enrolling. I also en-gaged with classmates and upper class students about their in-teractions with professors, personality-wise and material-wise. I got good grades because I majored in a subject that interested me. There are few people that do well in a major that does not interest them. Although my major was Economics, I minored in Management and Organization. I took Marketing, Accounting, Finance, and Management classes.

Taking a heavy course load in high school prepared me for a heavy load in college. If you don't know how to study (which is fine because a lot of people go to college without the proper study skills) you should definitely take a study skills class your freshman year so you aren't trying to play catch-up down the line. The key to having a successful semester is to take a mix of major and/or minor classes along with fun/intriguing electives. You must have balance. Taking 4 mathematical economics courses with a science is a set-up to fail for most people. Try to take 3 core classes and 2 electives per semester.

Whenever I found something hard to understand, I would approach my teachers right away. This helped me get better grades because I better understood the material, and it also helped me build relationships with my teachers, which benefited me personally. I was asked to be an Economics tutor at the end of my sophomore year. I was recommended for several merit scholarships all because of my relationships with teachers. Your professors want to help you, no matter how it seems, and the more you embrace them, the more they will help you and you will help yourself.

I believe in study groups, only after everyone has studied on their own. I have been in study groups that take place right after a lesson has been taught, and they are a waste of time if everyone is confused. As a tutor in college, I often led study groups and believe they are helpful. But if you don't study before you attend study group meetings, don't expect to leave knowing all of the answers.

When I arrived my freshman year, I signed up to be on the Dining Services Committee of the Student Government Association. I also became involved in the freshman honor society (Alpha

Lambda Delta) and served as treasurer. I had been treasurer for a few different organizations in high school so I stepped up to the plate at our first ALD meeting and offered to be secretary. The opportunity that forever changed my life was serving as President of the Student Government Association my senior year. In this office, I was truly able to make change. I planned two global immersion experiences for students who could not afford or did not want to study abroad for a whole semester. These two programs are still in effect at Spelman.

My freshmen year, I would go to information sessions when banks came on campus. I did a summer program with a bank my freshman year. After that, I spent every summer in NYC working on Wall Street. My senior year of college, I was asked to participate in a Marketing Competition on behalf of the NHL. I initially turned down the invite but after reading the case study decided that it would be fun. Eight months later, the Spelman team won the challenge, and I was absolutely in love with marketing.

I had already accepted a full time offer at the firm where I had interned over the summer. After a year and a half of working on Wall Street, I didn't feel fulfilled. The economy was in a deep recession at the time. I was lucky enough to land a position with a market leader doing Brand Innovation Marketing. I am absolutely in love with my job but I am extremely grateful for my time on Wall St. Through my summers and year and a half on Wall St., I gained a strong work ethic.

Everyone has passions; everyone has things about them that they do really well. Embrace those things and you will definitely find a career that suits you.

2008 Spelman College Graduate (3.6 GPA),
Brand Management

My parents instilled a sense of values of what an ideal or higher institution would be like, and I began to work towards this goal. I was never a good student prior to the 7th grade, but having the values of wanting to go to an esteemed institution pushed me to work hard thus allowing me to graduate valedictorian from junior high school, which ultimately led to my acceptance at one of the best local private high schools, The University of Chicago Laboratory Schools. I begin with this background because I really do believe that the earlier one can understand what type of institution is the right fit for them, the earlier you are able to cater your time to fulfilling the obligations to get into that school.

I wasn't a "wiz" in math or science and I liked being involved in the student body, enjoyed being on the track team, helping the year book, etc so I already had a knack for an "all around" type of school. I was also very social, and had many friends, so I knew very early on, that I was the "work hard, play hard" type. I continued this "work hard, play harder" strategy into high school.

Basically, my strategy was, if I stuck to a place whose culture mirrored my own values and personality, I couldn't go too wrong. I was clear that I didn't want to force myself into a place where I didn't feel I would already have a natural fit. In the end, I am grateful for all the steps that I've taken because I can truly say that those 4 years were some of the well-spent years of my life. I spent no time acclimating and changing to an environment that was completely opposite to me, and I was able to quickly assimilate in a community that supported me, and worked WITH my fundamental personality and values. University is a time to foster yourself, and exploit the resources that are made available to you.

The quarter system truly allowed you to sample a multitude of classes, without being afraid of making a wrong move. If you ventured into a class purely out of curiosity and it turned out to be your worst nightmare, it would end in 11 weeks! If, on the other hand, you ventured into a class, and ended up loving it. Well, there is the next quarter after that, and the one after that! You could explore all of your interests to whatever depth you desired.

Picking classes was always a stressful and tedious process. The single greatest factor in helping me select classes was having a strong and consistent academic advisor. At this age (and indeed at all points in life, but especially at this age), "you don't know what you don't know." So speaking with someone who can guide you and open your mind to new avenues…in other words, pairing your "half aspirations" and "half ideas" to concrete classes and paths is a valuable gift! Having a strong advisor to sit with you and help you think out your ideas is an absolute must to using your time most effectively. Even professors can become strong influencers in opening your eyes to classes, programs, and activities that can be of benefit to you. Always, always consult the help of those who have already taken the course!

I had a genuine interest in understanding the world and the policy that drove the political world. That is why I ultimately chose International Relations as my major. Now, onto good grades! There is no "secret" to getting good grades. Here are my suggestions in brief. First, PICK CLASSES YOU HAVE AN INTEREST IN. It is very easy to succeed at something you already have a vested interest in learning more about. It is very hard to engage in something you absolutely hate. I was Pre-Med when I entered

Stanford and was CERTAIN I would become a doctor. The first quarter I took organic chemistry and absolutely hated every second of it. I would spend hours upon hours in the library, hours upon hours in study groups, and I still managed to get only a C in this class. If this was the case, it was a pretty good indication that Pre Med wasn't exactly cut out for me, UNLESS, I was willing to stick it through, and I certainly wasn't! So the key to a good GPA is definitely to pick classes that you are interested in. WORK HARD. STUDY HARD. Nothing worthwhile comes without effort. The same is true of good grades.

The last and, perhaps, equally important with the point made above is GET TO KNOW YOUR PROFESSORS. I was never ever shy about office hours. Furthermore, I never hesitated to engage while in class. Don't be a passenger towards your classroom education. If the approach is to be a passenger, your grades will almost certainly reflect this "out of your hands" nature as well. You'll feel disconnected with not only the content of the class, but the outcome of the class as well. Engaging with professors is the absolute best way to ensure good grades. (It's true, professors are human too and they like students who are engaged. They like students who are interested in what they are interested in. After all, they've spent years and years and years studying whatever their profession is, why shouldn't you show interest in their work, and indeed, their LIFE!).

Being involved with professors is the key to not only succeeding in class, but really feeling engaged in work. I liked classes where I felt the expectation of the teacher. Where they encouraged me to succeed and I in turn, succeeded.

As I mentioned above, I was ALWAYS in professor's office like it was my second home. The first reason is professors are focused on ONE thing in class: GET THE INFORMATION OUT. They will address questions, and resolve concerns and the like, but their entire agenda for that time is: GET INFORMATION OUT THERE. In office hours, that is the EXACT OPPOSITE. Their ONLY DESIRE and agenda in offices hours is to get you to understand EVERYTHING they were talking about. And if they need to spend 1, 2, 3, 4 hours explaining to you in multiple sessions, a good professor will definitely make the time. They liked students who took an interest in their work, and for a student to go out of his way, is a special thing. So I always used office hours. It is a great thing! Study groups can honestly make or break a course. Sometimes there are classes that are so difficult, or so painful to get through because you absolutely hate everything that is coming out of the professor's mouth, that without the help and support of others, the work is not going to happen. Or at least, if the work happens, it's shabby and incomplete. Organic Chemistry was the most difficult course I have ever taken in my entire life. It was insanely difficult. And I honestly would not have passed this course, had I not spent ample time engaging with classmates to understand it from their perspective. I learned this after the first test. I completely bombed it and realized that the way I was studying and interpreting the material, was not the way the professor expected me to understand it. This realization came out of a meeting with the professor. Having the support of people who don't think like me was key. It helped me put things into a different perspective and ultimately saved me from failing this course and having to take it over again!! In statistics, I used study groups as well. But this time, I just simply hated what I was looking at. So on every homework assignment (which was due every week), I worked in a group to simply get me through it!

In terms of balancing the academic load, this is one of the most difficult feats for a college student who is CORRECTLY applying himself. If you find it easy to balance everything, then you SERIOUSLY need to reexamine why you are in school and how you are spending this invaluable time. I am among those who believe that you must be so busy, it requires EFFORT to balance your time and schedule. This is the only way to truly get everything out of university that you need to prepare you for the 'real world.'

Like many things in life, there is no "secret" to how to balance the academic load. It requires a keen eye to what's ultimately important to you. Nothing comes for free, and time is a limited resource. Ultimately it comes down to understanding what it most important to you, and more importantly, the UTILITY you get from pursuing a certain path. Two degrees won't make you any more qualified than a person who has one. But perhaps this was the best way for you to spend your time, because you were genuinely interested in the subject. Thus, balancing really is about understanding yourself, and ensuring that you are applying this understanding to an agenda that mirrors your interests.

Managing personal finances is an art that, if you can master, will never fail to let you down! In my freshmen year I received only 5% of the cost of school in scholarship. By sophomore year this was increased by several thousand to around 10% of the cost, at which point, my family was no longer able to pay for further financial aid due to our own economic difficulties. So, I essentially went from not having to worry about any payments for school because I thought it would be covered, to be throwing into the "fire pit," and having to cover a huge gap of 35k plus. My family gave me the option of attending a local state school that they could afford, but of course, having gotten into Stanford I absolutely refused this option. By junior year, roughly 80% of my tuition was covered, with the rest delegated by student loans and by senior year, almost 95% of my tuition was paid for. So, I guess you could say that in many ways, I was fortunate and lucky, but I also made my case very clear, and was willing to take the steps, for better or worse, to accommodate a situation that could work for me.

But I also was not shy about contributing through the federal work study program. I strategically chose to work at the career service center, because it accomplished several things that the other jobs didn't. First it had great pay, with long term career trajectory. I was promised a position as a career counselor for every year that I was on campus, which got rid of the headache of having to find a new occupation every year. Second, it was at the career service center, which was the hub of corporate full-time jobs and internships, as well as informational centers and anything related to careers and internships. Working there allowed me to see all of the opportunities coming through our school, first hand It also allowed me to have access to the library, which was a great study location for writing papers and getting things done at night.

The most important campus relationships are friends. These are the people going through the same experience, the people living and eating with you. These are people you can forge unforgettable bonds with for the rest of your life. In retrospect, I really wish I had spent more energy exerting and forging stronger friendships. While, I came out with several good friends which will last a life time, I know that I could have spent more time being on campus, instead of caught up with friends from the past. This is my only "regret" if I had any. It is always important to forge strong ties with any person who could play the advisor role in your life. Having a solid network of advisors, who can guide you to the correct path and inform you about opportunities and a cost/benefit analysis to any particular step, is key. These are the relationships I always sought and this always helped the most. For example, I had a really strong relationship with an academic advisor who helped guide me to my major in international relations. I had a strong advisor for classes and advisors in the spiritual realm that helped in guiding my life to balance everything out. I am calling them "advisors" here, but they really became strong friendships.

In terms of leadership roles, I chose roles that were limited to what really spoke to me. I was president of a religious organization. I was confident in my leadership qualities in class, and in my ability to get things done outside of extracurricular activities, such as studying abroad, or applying to various leadership academies or leadership fellowships. I focused on what gave me a sense of fulfillment. I was on the Stanford Judicial Panel Pool, which was a body of Student Affairs that voted on cases where students broke the honor code or student code of conduct. I enjoyed feeling the sense of responsibility for upholding the schools high ethical and moral standard, and at the same time, felt that it spoke to my core values, which was to act and conduct myself at all times in a way that is harmonious with moral values.

Finding a career that works with who you are as a person is one of the most challenging and gruesome undertakings that any college student, or recent graduate has. It is not easy, in the slightest, to find a career where you genuinely feel a sense of satisfaction from your core. A lot of the times, "what is right for us" or the "path we are supposed to take," takes precedent over listening to what we really want. After much introspection, I had discovered that I enjoyed the banking industry. Of course the compensation was a key component to my decision, but I was aware at the time that compensation was one factor that really made the difference in my personal sense of fulfillment. After dedicating myself to the banking path, and completing an internship at a Wall Street firm, I finally obtained what I thought would be the golden nugget: a full-time offer. I ended up turning down this offer in search of a deeper sense of fulfillment. I realized, through the experience, that I didn't simply want to just get paid. I wanted more. I wanted a platform where I would spend my time increasing my skills, and building upon the international scope I had spent so many days learning about. I ended up finding an amazing opportunity to work abroad for an oil and gas company that fit many of the criteria I had set out for myself. I can genuinely say that I have a true sense of fulfillment as I am tasked with building an entire division of the company from the bottom up, all by myself. There is nothing more rewarding than seeing the fruit of your labor improve the quality of something, be it a company, community or even relationship.

Having said all of this, I will say that the ultimate key, I believe, to having found this career, was in my unabashed declaration to try absolutely anything and everything. I did not shy away from any small inkling to try a path. I thus, interned in all of the areas I ever had interest in, including real estate development, organizational development, finance, U.S. government, and sales. These were all areas that had intrigued me in some shape or form, so I decided to try absolutely every avenue so that I could be absolutely confident that I had done everything to satisfy my curiosity as to what that particular career segment was like. I didn't want to have any regrets or thoughts about, "maybe I should have chosen this or that field." I wanted to know first hand, that I tried the field and I either liked it or hated it so that I could move forward boldly and confident onto the next opportunity. This I think was the ultimate key to finding a career I enjoy.

2008 Stanford University Graduate (3.6 GPA), Internal Controller

COLLEGE ACTION PLAN
FOR SUCCESS

We have detailed a Campus Action Plan that should be implemented as you begin your journey to a successful college experience:

- ☐ Get settled in your housing dorm/apartment. Meet roommates, maintain an open-minded, welcoming and friendly posture.

- ☐ Visit the financial aid/registrar's office to confirm receipt of tuition payments, scholarships, financial aid and/or stud ent loans.

- ☐ Verify participation in meal/health plan.

- ☐ Establish relationships with upperclassmen. This can be accomplished with individuals in your dorm, campus organizations, and resident advisors.

☐ Determine fraternities, sororities and other campus organizations to get involved in.

☐ Determine if you need a part-time job or work study and explore options and suggested recommendations.

☐ Review schedule to make sure you have appropriate classes and a balanced load.

☐ Purchase/acquire books/other materials required for classes. Please be aware that there are internet sites and the campus bookstore where you can buy used books.

☐ Obtain appropriate time management tools (daily planner or electronic calendar) and create a daily routine that incorporates your class schedule, study time, campus club meetings, study group sessions and personal interests.

☐ Familiarize yourself with class location to guarantee timely arrival.

☐ Predetermine the grades you expect to receive for each class and plan your schedule to allocate appropriate study time.

☐ Join or initiate a study group in each class.

☐ Review professor/TA office hours and schedule an appointment to visit each professor/TA by the end of second week.

APPENDIX

Research Insights

In our research, we asked 3rd and 4th year college students across the country questions about their college experience. They have openly shared the successes and frustrations they faced and dealt with early in their college experience…some of the same concerns and fears you may have. By using the wisdom and experiences shared, you will be off to a great start or improve how you finish and graduate, having had an amazing college experience. Excerpts from the survey are catalogued here.

What impact has attending college had on your ability to be successful?

Attending college has been paramount to my success. I have grown leaps and bounds in ways I don't think I can yet fully appreciate. It has been a phenomenal experience.

4th year Northwestern student

It has opened my eyes to careers I would have never considered. It has also opened doors for me in industries that require a high level of achievement and performance, which are usually closed to people without a college degree.

3ʳᵈ year Boston University student

Attending college has provided me with endless resources and opportunities. It has exposed me to things that I would not have known about or been able to do otherwise. And I have had experiences that will last and affect me for a lifetime.

3ʳᵈ year Florida State Univ. student

College is an unbelievable and invaluable experience. Being in a learning environment and exposed to different people, ideas, and opportunities, success in one's true calling becomes easy if you work hard and believe you can succeed.

4ᵗʰ year Univ. of Southern CA student

College has really increased my self-awareness. I have been exposed to a variety of programs and opportunities that I wouldn't have known about had I not been a student. I've traveled to wonderful places with organizations that I've joined, and I've made a lot of really close friends.

4ᵗʰ year Univ. of Georgia student

College has helped me to think more critically about various issues that I may not personally agree with. By doing this, I can better understand people and be more understanding when I meet people from different backgrounds or who have different opinions than my own, allowing for many new opportunities to come my way.

3rd year Spelman College student

College has equipped me with multiple toolsets, skills, and a broadened perspective that is absolutely invaluable. Specifically, my reading comprehension, analytical skills, and writing abilities have increased tremendously.

3rd year Amherst Student

It has allowed me to meet new people with similar and different interests from mine, yet with great ambitions. As a result, it has created a wider platform of people from which I can learn. Going to college has opened up significant opportunities for career choices/paths. It has also given me a network of motivated and successful individuals that I did not previously have.

3rd year Georgetown student

What do you now know or wish you had known before you started college and what advice would you give high school students preparing to enter college?

Develop relationships with your professors as early as your freshman year (and make sure to maintain them as you advance in your college career). They will come in handy later when you need a mentor to reach out to, career guidance, or even a letter of recommendation. Remember that you are in college to obtain a degree and graduate. Being involved in student organizations is very important, but you always need to keep track of your academics and do not let your GPA slide because later, when you accumulate a lot of hours, it will be very difficult to change. Although it may not seem so at the moment, the classes you take your first two years (all your basics) will probably be the easiest classes you take in college and you need to take advantage of this to build a strong foundation for your GPA. Create a budget. I cannot emphasize this enough: you need to understand that you are on your own now and have to deal with things that you probably never worried about before (rent, bills, groceries, etc.). Do monitor your health closely. Just because you are not at home please don't forget to keep up with yearly routine physical exams. Do be aware of the freshman 15, tracking your calorie intake, proper exercise, and trying to sleep at least 5-8 hours every night is very important.

4th year Univ. of Texas, McComb student

I wish I [had] known how to be a more effective studier and I wish I [had] known the value of group work (working with others to accomplish tasks). I would tell high school students to come to college with an open mind, try new things, don't be afraid to ask for help when you need [it], and try not to be involved with everything--just pick a couple of things you can be the most effective at and focus on those. Also, work on developing good study habits ASAP!

4ᵗʰ year Univ. of Georgia student

I wish I [had] known from the beginning that I should aim for Latin Honors. It seems like such a small thing but coming into college, I was satisfied with A's and B's. I never thought I could be at the top of my class. From the beginning, I should have believed that I could be at the top. College is a new beginning for everyone; my advice to students would be to leave old baggage behind (as much as possible) and then sit down and decide what your academic and personal growth goals are for college, and go after them. Don't doubt. Just do it.

4ᵗʰ year Duke Univ. student

College is about exploring, really. Every interaction is another piece of the mosaic that will be not just a great career, but a great life. Pay attention to the surprises (e.g., that kid in the hallway who no one talks to; that Asian American dance group you would never have gone to watch; that professor whose lecture was unusually compelling): they are usually clues to the larger picture. If you commit to following these clues, you will often find gold!

4th year Stanford student

Apply for as many scholarships as you can; my personal experience was that local scholarships (from your school district, your city, or those specifically targeted to your school, etc.) are much easier to obtain than national ones. That is not to say that national scholarships are impossible to get, it is just that the pool of applicants for these scholarships is a lot bigger and, therefore, these are a lot more competitive to obtain. Also, do continue to apply for scholarships once you are in college.

4th year Univ. of Texas, McComb student

When I was in high school, I probably wasn't the best student and I did not really have any clue about what I wanted. I would suggest taking classes in what interests you the most, and it's okay if over time your interests change. I wanted to be an aerospace engineer and then I wanted to go to business school to study finance. I would also suggest that as a freshman you start building relationships with alumni of your school or school-related organizations and professionals in the industry you may want to enter. You should try to find as much information about careers, and what people do on a daily basis in their respective fields. If you want to go into finance then you should start reading the Wall St. Journal earlier rather than later in college

4ᵗʰ year NYU student

You do not have to know exactly what you want to do upon entering school. It is okay to wait upon declaring a major, opting to take classes, and getting involved in organizations you think you would enjoy first. College is for discovering who you are; you aren't expected to know who that is at 18.

3ʳᵈ year Fisk Univ. student

The advice that I would give to high school students would be to make sure they have grounded themselves with great study skills and to be prepared to read, read, read! Practice writing essays and write as much as you can because it will only help you in college.

4ᵗʰ year Connecticut College student

I knew that Ivy Leagues or more prestigious schools were great for the education, but I had no real desire to attend one. Now, the more I meet people and the more programs I'm involved in, the more I realize that those schools have a greater impact on my future. I would tell college students to go to the best school they can get into; take advantage of the resources available to you and make the most of each opportunity; NETWORK, NETWORK, NETWORK and cultivate relationships; get internships; don't just focus on the "here and now;" also focus on preparing for your future; ENJOY COLLEGE because it really is the TIME OF YOUR LIFE, but it goes by VERY FAST."

3rd year student at Florida State University

When you are in high school, teachers and of classes are chosen for you. So at that time, you have no idea of your learning style, best study method, or best note taking skills. You are just doing what you're being told. In college, I found myself lost, and it took me two semesters to find the best resource for selecting teachers (www.ratemyprofessor.com); understand my learning style; and realize there was more to studying than just memorization. Also, if I had a clearer understanding of classes beforehand, there are quite a few classes I wouldn't have taken.

4th year Clemson Univ. student

What three things did you struggle with during your first two years of college?

1. *Changing majors*
2. *New level of academic difficulty*
3. *Making new friends*

4th *year Stanford Univ. student*

1. *Illness (without parental support)*
2. *Managing time (any given week I had more homework than there w[ere] hours in the week to do and learning what readings are less important is necessary)*
3. *Balancing social life and academic life*

3rd *year Univ. of Chicago student*

1. *Time management*
2. *Getting the grade*
3. *Reaching out for help*

4th *year Georgetown student*

1. *Learning to deal with different personalities*
2. *Budgeting my money*
3. *Overcoming fear of rejection*

4ᵗʰ year Univ. of Georgia student

1. *Not knowing who to talk to about struggling in classes*
2. *Not feeling like I belonged at this college*
3. *Balancing extracurriculars, academics and rest*

4ᵗʰ year Stanford Univ. student

1. *Class reading requirements*
2. *New culture*
3. *Being separated from my family*

3ʳᵈ year Amherst College student

1. *Involvement, since I'm a commuter student*
2. *Finding a balance between school and work*
3. *Learning to prioritize all of the things I had to do, given my limited amount of time*

3ʳᵈ year Univ. of Southern CA student

1. *Time management*
2. *Seeking out campus resources*
3. *Career Planning*

4th *year Univ. of Virginia student*

1. *Academic rigor of college material*
2. *Writing skills*
3. *Adjusting socially to college life*

3rd *year Dartmouth student*

1. *Financial Security*
2. *Not being the "leader" (student council, captain)*
3. *Writing succinctly*

4th *year Claremont McKenna College student*

1. *Identity as a minority on campus*
2. *Utilizing people who cared for me (friends and mentors)*
3. *Feeling comfortable and confident in pursuing my passions*

3rd *year Stanford Student*

As a first generation college student, what impact did this have at the beginning of your college experience?

I think that being first generation means that I did not have much guidance with the college admissions process, but also with navigating through University resources and a general sense of direction.

4ᵗʰ Year Yale Univ. student

I think it gave me more drive and determination to succeed, especially because I know that there are a lot of people "cheering" for me. I always have felt like I've been ahead and progressive even though I had no one to directly go before me and say this is what you do/don't do.

3ʳᵈ year FSU student

Not much of an impact.

4ᵗʰ year Hamilton College student

When I came to college, I did not know what to expect, and neither did my parents. At times I do feel like my peers are ahead of the game, but I do think that because of the support I received at school, I was able to succeed.

4ᵗʰ year Washington Univ. student

At the beginning of my college experience, I was not really at the standards of other students that have parents or older brothers that know about the college lifestyle. Instead I was faced with figuring everything out by myself and on my own since I am 5 hrs and 30 minutes away from home when traveling by bus.

3ʳᵈ year Ithaca College student

I was very nervous leaving home and being on my own. My parents have never experienced this so they had no advice to give me except to be a good student and watch out for myself. In the beginning I struggled with the workload but eventually I learned from my mistakes.

3ʳᵈ year Cornell Univ. student

There was no real support system at home because the concept of college was unfamiliar to my parents.

4ᵗʰ year UT Austin student

What value does/did budgeting have on your college experience?

Budgeting money can really affect your mood. I try to spend money conservatively, and then have a good time when I feel I've deserved it by doing well on a test or something similar.

4th year MIT student

Having a budget kept me in line with carefree spending (I love to shop) and it allowed me to see where I was spending the most money. Also, it encouraged me to save more.

3rd year FSU student

It is simple, save as much as you can and definitely don't spend more than what you have. If you take out loans, focus in school! The hours that you waste in a meaningless school job could be better invested studying in order for you to ultimately obtain greater returns after college.

4th year Stony Brook Univ. student

I have budgeted my entire life, so budgeting in college was nothing new and only furthered my appreciation for the things I have and what people give me.

3rd year Amherst College student

Money wasn't too much of an option. Just being a good steward of scholarship money. I had enough for books, food, clothes, and basic living. Financially, I just used common sense to avoid wasteful spending or getting into debt by living beyond my means.

3rd year Fisk University student

Budgeting is great because it helps you develop discipline [which] also includes other positive things. I try to reward myself for a good job, and not reward myself for a bad grade. Creating my own incentives has worked well to motivate me to try harder, and grow. You need to learn how to budget especially when you graduate. I actually just tried to create a budget for myself for the next 3 years. I think it's important to always stay on top of your own finances.

4th year NYU student

How many math courses have you taken and share the value of those courses or the impact of not taking math courses?

I have taken three semesters of math - stats, single and multi variable calculus. I feel that these classes have not had an impact in my life but employers are looking for these classes and they help you become more competitive.

3rd year Berkeley student

In everything there is math. My math coursework has enabled me to expand the way I approach problem solving in all disciplines.

3rd year Univ. of Chicago student

I have taken 7 math courses. Their value has been new ways of approaching problems and the ability to utilize real data and numbers to show why an idea is reasonable or not.

4th year Univ. of Southern CA student

The reason why I did not take more is because as a finance and economics major, most of my classes are math based and were built off of my math classes.

4th year Univ. of Buffalo student

I have taken one math course - Basic Statistics. Statistics would have been more valuable if I had performed better. I'm thinking I might retake it or take another introductory course in statistical methods of research. Not taking math classes has made it difficult to understand research in all of my classes. I would suggest students take at least one or two math classes in college. Math should be a requirement taken during your freshman year.

3rd year Stanford student

I have taken two math classes and they have been a tremendous help in my classes that focus on finance, economics and accounting.

4th Babson College student

I have taken a few math courses and they have allowed me to realize how hard I must work in order to develop my quantitative skills.

3rd year Amherst College student

I've taken 3 math courses and many course that rely heavily on math. As a result, I feel very comfortable with numbers and I have the tools for solving problems analytically.

4th year MIT student

What impact has leadership involvement on campus had on your college experience?

Being involved on campus has given me experience in working with others, managing my time, and being responsible for work that affects more than just me (schoolwork only affects you).

4th year MIT student

Leadership involvement on campus has made me aware of my strengths and weaknesses. It has also enabled me to build relationships with my peers and differentiate myself from others. Moreover, it has shown me how to disagree with others in a tactful and civil manner.

4th year Claremont McKenna College

Leadership roles on campus have allowed me to realize my limitations, to know what I can achieve when I put my mind to it, and to witness how my actions and words impact others.

3rd year Univ. of Southern CA student

Being involved in various organizations has allowed me to discover my leadership style. It has also allowed me to be more directed in my future pursuits. Even things I participated in that I didn't like have helped me hone in on the things that I do enjoy.

4th year Duke Univ. student

Leadership involvement on campus has given me responsibility outside of my coursework. In particular, my leadership position has given me a mentor and made me a student who is looked up to as a minority leader. I have a sense of duty to others now, as well as to myself. Being responsible for others has given me motivation, and gratification that helps me in facing academic challenges.

3rd year Stanford student

I learned to use my leadership position to bring together a tight knit community that works together for a common purpose.

3rd year Simmons College student

What comes to mind when you think about integrity? Share circumstances or situations where you felt integrity was an issue.

Integrity is very important. A lot of situations require trust among teammates, and dealing with people that have a lot of integrity is very reassuring.

4th year MIT student

Integrity means sticking to your morals and ethics regardless of the situation. You must face the consequences of your actions.

4th year Northwestern Student

Integrity is doing the right thing. Treating yourself and others how you would want to be treated and with their best interests in mind. Always treat others with respect.

4th year Univ. of Southern CA student

Honesty and truthfulness. It might be difficult to maintain integrity when you're in an academically difficult situation. But just remember that [the] grades you earn on your own are more satisfying.

4th year Stanford Univ. student

Integrity is doing the right thing even when you don't want to.

3rd Florida State Univ. student

Helping friends [who are] struggling with a problem set when collaboration is not allowed but they are failing the class. - trying to balance being a helpful person with being a person of integrity

4th year Stanford student

How did you create or decide on your own "personal brand"? Describe traits and characteristics of your "personal brand" and what impact it has had on your college experience?

I decided my personal brand would be the characteristics/ traits I've had since I was a child. I've always been a person that sticks to my guns; I say what I mean and mean what I say. I've never settled for anything less than I want and I've always been the advice-giver. These characteristics describe who I am as a person and were immediately recognized in my friends, by professors, organization members, and team members. They understand that I am dedicated and dependable and that I won't stop working until I'm satisfied with the results and all goals are met. It's really made college satisfying knowing that people see me this way and are more inclined to work with me/befriend me.

4th year Univ. of Georgia student

I decided on my own "personal brand" after I learned that it's not what you do, but how well you do it that matters in becoming successful. The skills of my personal brand include empathy, interpersonal, and listening skills.

3rd year Stanford student

My personal brand is always growing and changing. But I have identified characteristics that I always want to be associated with me. For example, honesty, dependability, hard work ethic, intelligence; these are all traits that I work hard to embody. As you grow older, you realize that the way you present yourself to others impacts almost every facet of your life. Increasing the value of your personal brand creates opportunities and connections. For that reason, it is something I will always work on.

3rd year Amherst College student

I knew that I did not have an internship and I also knew I was not coming from the best school and did not have the highest GPA but I am funny, I had a diverse childhood and I am able to hold strong conversation so I used that in conjunction with my campus leadership to make people want to speak with me more.

3rd year Florida State Univ. student

I thought about what my family, friends and colleagues would say about me if they were to be asked [about] my strengths. Once I identified those characteristics, I thought about my experiences that reflected them. For example, I am very personable, disciplined and [a] hard worker. Proof, I moved to the US 4 years ago- with little to no knowledge of English- and I have lived in 4 different regions of North America. During this time I have been able to learn the language, immerge myself in the culture of these regions and succeed academically.

4th year Stony Brook Univ. student

I understood I had to make myself distinguishable. I realized which traits got people to speak well about me and I capitalized on them. I was able to stand out among my peers in settings outside the classroom, which had a significant impact on every aspect of my college life, not just socially. For example, word had spread that I was able to fund-raise a sizable amount of scholarship money for a student group I was involved in, and I was contacted by an alumni organization to help out with its fundraising efforts.

4th year Stanford student

Why did you choose your major and does your major support your current career aspirations?

I chose to major in public relations because I have been persuading my parents to take my side of a situation since I was very young. I felt I had strong writing skills, and at Hampton University, they have a very strong PR program and a great school of journalism and communications. This falls in line with my career aspiration. To be in the marketing or advertising industry, you have to have strong communication skills. I feel that having this different major will also set me apart from other MBA candidates that take the traditional route of undergraduate business degrees.

3rd year Hampton Univ. student

I knew I wanted to be involved in something within the business world. Economics was the most appropriate choice given all the majors offered at my liberal arts college.

4th year Hamilton College student

It felt like the natural choice once I started. I honestly don't remember choosing it. And it does somewhat lie within my career aspirations. Business and economics are such flexible disciplines; it can be applied in almost any situation.

4th year Cornell student

I choose my major because I love creating ideas and bringing them to life. This is why I chose marketing. I chose the College of Business because my mother obtained her degrees, undergrad and MBA in business. She was able to make a lot of money but still be readily available when I needed her.

3rd year Univ. of Illinois student

I chose a finance major because it was my major in high school and I enjoyed it. I picked up my second major in economics because I thought it would complement finance and enable me to be well rounded. I felt that business and economics will help me in any field.

4th year Univ. of Buffalo student

Look for our companion book: <u>Coached for Success! Millennials in the Marketplace</u>. This book provides the seven success strategies for establishing yourself as a top performer in the Workplace.

ACKNOWLEDGMENTS

Coached for Success! a powerful partnership of different, yet equal strengths. WOW! is what came to mind when we completed this labor of love. Partnering together brought out the best in each of us. We both had books in us and our friendship, trust, and faith allowed us to become a formidable force and together create this body of work. God, we thank you for endless possibilities and divinely connecting and equipping us.

Two husbands, seven children, homework, afterschool activities, and full time jobs…how did we do? Inspiration, encouragement, discipline and lots of laughter!

To my husband Ray, my voice of reason, thank you doesn't begin to express my adoration and appreciation. Your unwavering support and commitment is a testament to your character. After 16 years of marriage, your love remains genuine and fresh. Your keen insight and incredible appetite for reading and staying current on market trends added valuable perspective to this project. Hearing your voice consistently and unrelenting telling me to…write, write, write, remained in my consciousness and carried me through. Thank you for allowing me to eat meals at the computer and helping the kids understand that mommy was "working".

To Ryan, Carly and Carson, my three beautiful, spirited and funny daughters, you inspire me to be more than "mommy". To Hamilton, my son and encourager, you never forget to ask me about my day and stick around to hear the answer.

To my mom, thank you for your wisdom and answering life's questions with the simplest, yet most insightful phrase "keep living". To Robin, you have been an amazing friend. We have walked through the seasons of life together and learned to *blow kisses*. To Damon, my friend of more than 20 years thanks for always providing clarity, truth and wisdom. To Romi, thank you for your creativity and friendship. To Gayle, you kept us on task, constantly reminding us to get it done. Thanks for your prayers and discernment.

Thank you to Angela, Alexis, Cheridah, Phyllis, Jeffrey, Leslie (my father in-law), and so many others who encouraged me, listened to my stories and said "you should write a book". Thank you to Tomell, Ashley, Ryan, Kimberly and all the other talented and gifted students and professionals I have had the pleasure of coaching.

Last, but certainly not least, my partner Rishal, I could not have done this without you. Thank you for being my friend. I love your zeal for life and adventure.

Valerie

Kenny thanks for always being there to support me throughout our 16 years of marriage. Your willingness to always allow me to pursue my dreams has been so inspiring. Your technical assistance from the beginning of the CFS project made the launch so much easier. Thanks for always being there to cover on the long nights when we plugged away on this project. I couldn't have done it without you. I love you dearly.

For my three wonderful K's (Kennedy, Ken, and Kendall), thanks so much for your patience with mommy as we worked tirelessly to complete this project. You encourage me to work hard in all that I do. Your willingness to help around the house really made completing the process so much easier. I love you dearly and hope this book inspires you to succeed in all of your educational endeavors. Jazmine and Benjamin, my gifted niece and nephew thanks for the inspiration to share success strategies with other college students. I am so proud of your college success at Spelman and Iowa State, keep up the great work.

Valerie, it's been quite a ride. I thank God that you were the partner destined to travel with me on this journey. Here's to completing the first project of many my friend! Your ability to "Valerize" truly amazes me.

Beth, Horizon Christian Staff, RCFM family, my prayer partners, Douglas family, Smith family, Carpenter family, Browne-Sanders family, Dana, Tony, Sonya, Val, Brian at Cre843, Dinkins/Green/Lillie family, Jones/Simmons/Stanciel family, First Editing, and all of my friends, thanks to each of you for doing your part to support this project. I bless God for your willingness to help make the process smoother, and the dream a reality. Finally, to all of my MLT students, RCFM mentees, GLUE fellows, BH youth, my prayer partners Felicia F./Felicia P., my dear friend Anucha, and NU family thanks for being the inspiration to write this book. Your input was invaluable. I love all of you!

Rishal

SELECTED REFERENCES

Behman, John. "*Got Work? College Graduates Face Toughest Market in Years*." Available from http://www.abcnews.go.com/Business/story, Internet; accessed Jan. 2010.

Carey, Kevin, Hess, Frederick M., Kelly, Andrew P., and Schneider, Mark, American Enterprise Institute Study: "*Diplomas and Dropouts: Which Colleges Actually Graduate Their Students (and Which Don't)*," Available from http://www.aei.org/event/100065 , June 2009; Internet; accessed Dec, 2009.

Carey, Kevin, The Education Trust Report: "*A Matter of Degrees: Improving Graduation Rates in Four-Year Colleges and Universities*," Available from http://www.edtrust.org, Internet; accessed Dec, 2009.

Hamilton, Gary, "A Brief Bio," 2008, Internet; accessed Dec 2009.

Hardt, David Leon, "Colleges are failing in graduation rates," *New York Times*, Sept. 2009, Available from http://www.nytimes.com, Internet; accessed Jan, 2010.

Hill, Scott, WireTap Magazine, "Swimming With Student Loan Sharks", September 27, 2007, Available from http://www.wiretapmag.org/education, Internet; accessed Jan, 2010.

Iorg, Dr. Jeff, "Foundations for Integrity in Leadership," June 23, 2008, Available from http://jeffiorg.com/feed/insights.atom, Internet; accessed Dec, 2009.

Sallie Mae's National Study of Usage Rates and Trends, "How Undergraduate Students Use Credit Cards," 2009, Available from http://www.salliemae.com, Internet; accessed Jan, 2010.

US Census Press Release, January 10, 2008, Available from http://www.census.gov/Press-Release, Internet; accessed Dec 2009.

Wikipedia definition of Common Sense, Available from http://en.wikipedia.org/wiki, Internet; accessed Dec 2009.

Websites:
Cornell.edu, Cost of attending Cornell University for a Georgia resident; Available from http://www.cornell.edu, Internet; accessed Jan 2010.

FSU.edu, Cost of attending Florida State University for a Georgia resident, Available from http://www.fsu.edu, Internet; accessed Jan 2010.

UGA.edu, Cost of attending Univ. of GA for Georgia resident, Available from http://www.uga.edu, Internet; accessed Jan 2010.

5881305R0

Made in the USA
Charleston, SC
16 August 2010